I0729799

# JÜRG STÜNZI

ROTOGRAPHY

OTOGRAPHYR

TOGRAPHYRO

OGRAPHYROT

GRAPHYROTO

# VORWORT

*Es wird hier eine neue, spezifische Art der Abbildung aufgezeigt: Abrollbilder oder Rotographien. Das vorliegende Buch erläutert meinen Weg, meine Experimente sowie meinen Bezug zu den rotographierten Objekten.*
*Das Aufnehmen von Panoramaphotos ist heute mit jedem Smartphone problemlos möglich. Anstelle der üblichen horizontalen Schwenkbewegung zur Erzeugung eines klassischen Panoramabildes kann die Kamera aber auch ganz anders geführt werden, in Kurven, in vertikaler oder paralleler Verschiebung. Was dann als Bild erzeugt wird, ist ein neues Universum des Sehens bzw. des Abbildens.*
*Anstatt diese Bilder als Artefakte zu verwerfen, habe ich mich ihnen mit Verwunderung zugewandt – und mit Bewunderung! Die nächste Überraschung war, dass es mir unter bestimmten Bedingungen gelang, ein Objekt mit der Kamera so aufzunehmen, dass ein kontinuierliches Abrollbild, eine Rotographie, entsteht. Dies war der Ausgangspunkt einer bisher acht Jahre dauernden Entdeckungsreise – durch eine Welt von Objekten und Symbolen des Alltäglichen. Sowohl Naturobjekte als auch Artefakte werden mit dieser speziellen Methodik einer neuen Wahrnehmung zugänglich gemacht. Sie werden, mit den Mitteln der Kamera, quasi zu neuartigen „unknown objects", virtuellen Skulpturen, gleichermassen bekannt und doch irritierend anders – stilisiert und ästhetisiert durch die Rotographie. Das Buch führt die Leserin und den Leser durch dieses gestalterische Experiment, beleuchtet Technik und Hintergründe und lädt zum Betrachten, zur Kontemplation der rotographischen Welt ein.*

*Thalwil, 17. April 2021*      *Jürg Stünzi*

# PREFACE

This book presents a new genre of photography – unrolled images or rotographies. In it I recount how my experiments with photography led me to discover this new field and explain what inspired me to work with the rotographed objects I have chosen for this book.
Today, any smartphone can take panoramic photos by panning horizontally or vertically along a straight line. However, in addition to the usual classic panoramic image, a camera can also be used to create a uniquely different kind of panoramic image by panning vertically or horizontally along a curved rather than a straight line. This generates a new world of perception and imaging. Instead of discarding these images, I viewed them with fascination and wonder and started to work explicitly with them. I was surprised how easily – under certain conditions – I was able to capture objects in such a way that a continuous unrolling image, a rotography, was created. This was the starting point for a journey of discovery through a world of everyday objects which has so far lasted eight years. Using this technique, both natural and man-made objects can be seen from a new perspective. The camera turns them into virtual sculptures which are at once familiar and unfamiliar. They are stylized and aestheticized by the process of rotography.
This book guides the reader through my creative journey, explains the techniques behind rotography and invites the reader to contemplate the world of rotography.

Thalwil 17 April 2021      Jürg Stünzi

# INHALT

IN T R O

N T R O I

T R O I N

R O I N T

O I N T R

# PANORAMA

Art evolves, encourages experimentation, breaks boundaries and attempts to master new challenges. In the visual arts, this means not only the discovery of new techniques and materials, be it in drawing, painting, or photography but also experimenting with size, area, space and movement. In short, spatial experimentation.
A pivotal moment in the evolution of the visual arts was the creation of gigantic circular images by the Irishman Robert Barker (1739–1806) to whom the invention of panoramas is attributed. The viewer stands in the center of a dome-shaped room in which an oversized cylindrical image is displayed and is immersed in a make-believe universe. According to contemporary reports, these novel installations induced in the viewer heightened sensations and feelings of euphoria. The enthusiasm with which these panoramas were received was similar to that later experienced during the early days of cinematography or to the current fascination with the exploration of virtual reality. In the 19th century, such circular installations became a new branch of the entertainment industry, displayed on a grand scale at a variety of venues such as fairs and world exhibitions. Murals up to fifteen meters high and more than a hundred meters long were created in cylindrical stages and circular buildings. The audience could indulge themselves in the illusion of being at the center of a grandiose scene. Since these panoramas were primarily considered to be a form of optical illusion (trompe-l'oeil), even a kind of fairground attraction, their artistic merit was considered to be of secondary importance. Nevertheless, one can hardly fail to be impressed by the level of accomplishment exhibited in these works of art.



# PANORAMA

*Kunst entwickelt sich, drängt zum Experimentieren, war und ist immer wieder auch der Versuch, Neues zu erobern und Grenzen zu sprengen. In den bildenden Künsten ist das nicht nur das Finden neuer Techniken und Materialien, sei es im Zeichnerischen, in der Malerei oder in der Photographie. Es war und ist auch das Experimentieren mit Grösse, Fläche, Raum und Bewegung.*
*Ein eindrückliches Sprengen des Rahmens war die Erfindung von Panoramen – eine dem Iren Robert Barker (1739–1806) zugeschriebene Präsentation von gigantischen Rundbildern: Der Betrachter steht im Zentrum einer überdimensionalen zylindrischen Bildkomposition, welche ihn in eine Scheinwelt versetzt. Was diese Anlagen damals an grossartigen Sinneseindrücken, Euphorie, ja magischen Momenten auslösten, ist in zeitgenössischen Berichten wiedergegeben: ein Begeisterungssturm, wie er später der Cinematographie zuteil wurde oder heute Präsentationen von Virtual Reality.*
*Solche Rundbilder-Anlagen wurden im 19. Jahrhundert zu einer Unterhaltungsindustrie, welche sich an Massenanlässen – von Jahrmärkten bis zu Weltausstellungen – in pompösen Ausmassen inszenierte.*
*Es entstanden bis zu 15 Meter hohe und mehr als 100 Meter lange Wandbilder in zylindrischen Schaubühnen und Rundbauten. Das Publikum konnte sich der Illusion hingeben, Teil und Mittelpunkt einer grandiosen Szene zu sein.*
*Da diese Panoramen als eine Sonderform der Effektmalerei, als optische Täuschung (Trompe-l'oeil) und Jahrmarkt-Volkskunst gelten, wird ihr kunstmalerischer Wert als eher zweitrangig eingestuft. Dennoch kann man sich des stupenden Eindrucks dieser Kunstwerke kaum entziehen.*

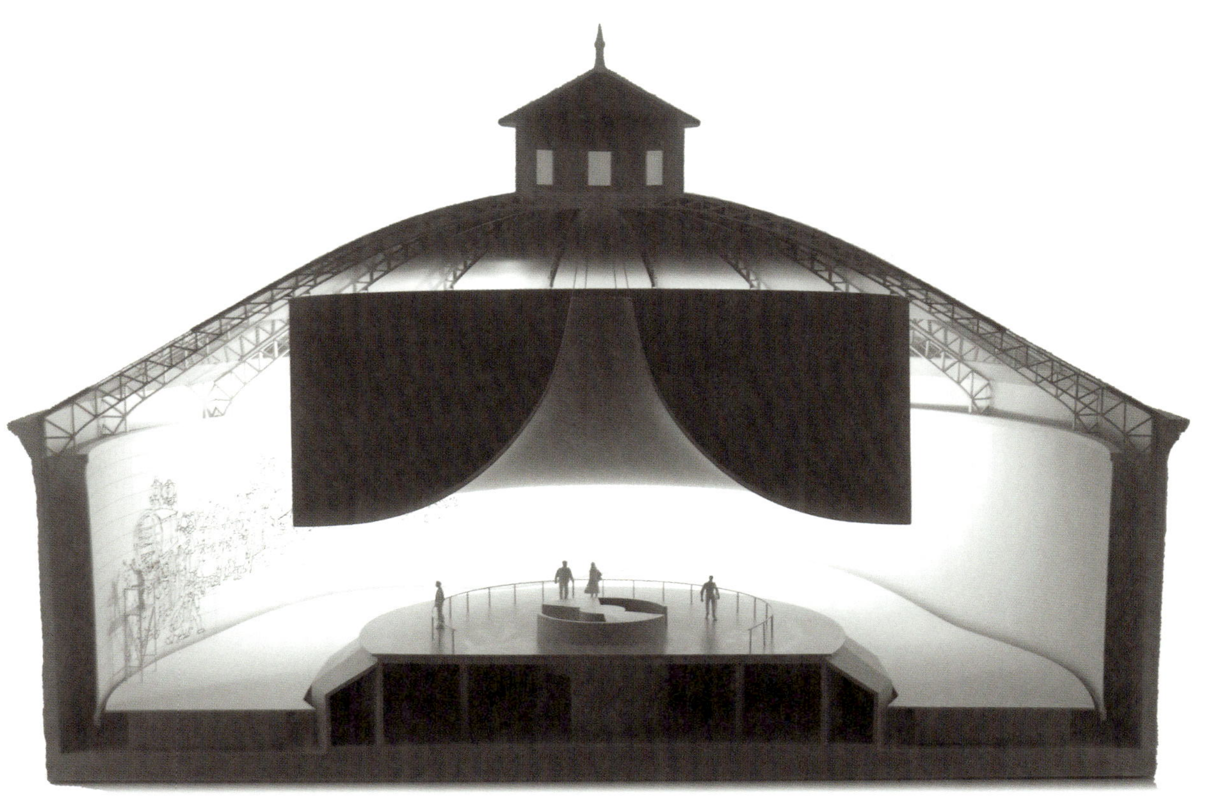

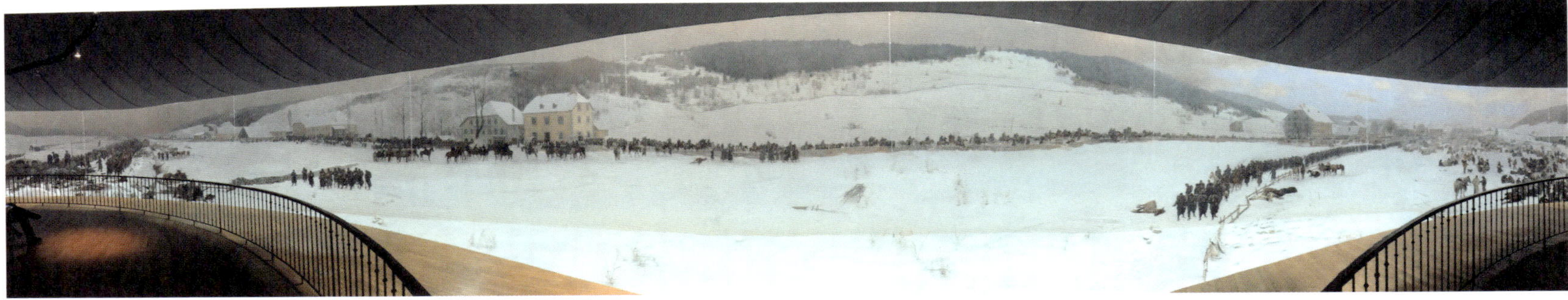

Bourbaki Panorama, Luzern: (oben) Schematische Darstellung der Anlage (Informationstafel zur Anlage); (unten) Ausschnitt des 1881 durch Edouard Castres geschaffenen Rundgemäldes.

Bourbaki Panorama, Lucerne, Switzerland: (top) Schematic representation of the complex; (bottom) Detail of the circular painting created in 1881 by Edouard Castres.

# ORIGINS

Even though the panoramas or circular painting installations were revolutionary, they were by no means unrelated to works of art of earlier epochs. A similar immersive impression was created by the magnificent images which were painted on the walls, ceilings and domes of many churches and palaces during the Renaissance. One striking example is the wall painting in Palazzo Te, a very well-preserved summer palace of Federico II Gonzaga in Mantua, Italy, from the 16th century.

Particularly famous is the Fall of the Giants room, where a monumental painting extends as a continuous pictorial motif over all four walls and the domed ceiling. The architect and painter Giulio Romano had the room designed in such a way that all corners (except those where the walls meet the floor) are rounded and therefore concealed by the painting and hardly perceptible to the viewer.

The overall impression is thus very similar to that of the panoramas of the 19th century.

The Fall of the Giants, painted between 1532 and 1535, is a Renaissance interpretation of a motif from Ovid's Metamorphoses. It shows the dramatic moment when Zeus puts down the uprising of the giants with thunder and lightning. The structure built out of boulders by the giants in order to storm the sky dramatically collapses and buries the rebels under stones and rubble.

(Source: According to the Italian description of the picture on site)

# URSPRUNG


*Die Panoramen oder Rundbilderanlagen waren revolutionär, aber keineswegs losgelöst von Kunstwerken früherer Epochen. Dieselbe Art von überwältigendem Gesamteindruck erzeugten auch die grossartigen Wand-, Decken- und Kuppelmalereien, welche in der Renaissance vielerorts in Kirchen und Palästen entstanden.*

*Als stringentes Beispiel dient hier die Wandmalerei im Palazzo Te, einem sehr gut erhaltenen Sommerpalast von Federico II. Gonzaga in Mantua (Italien) aus dem 16. Jahrhundert.*

*Besonders berühmt ist der Raum „Fall der Giganten", in dem sich ein monumentales Gemälde als zusammenhängendes Bildmotiv über alle vier Wände und die Kreuzkuppel erstreckt. Der Architekt und Maler Giulio Romano liess den Raum so bearbeiten und gestalten, dass alle Ecken (ausser denjenigen der Bodenfläche) abgerundet, durch die Malerei kaschiert und für den Betrachter kaum wahrnehmbar sind.*

*Der Gesamteindruck kommt damit demjenigen der Panoramen des 19. Jahrhunderts sehr nahe. Das Bild „Fall der Giganten" (zwischen 1532 und 1535) ist die Renaissance-Umsetzung eines Motivs aus Ovid's Metamorphosen. Es zeigt den dramatischen Moment, in dem Zeus mit Blitz und Donner den Aufstand der Riesen niederschlägt. Dramatisch kollabiert die von den Riesen aus Bergmassen und Gebäuden zur Erstürmung des Himmels errichtete Konstruktion und begräbt die Rebellen unter Fels und Schutt.*

*(Quelle: Nach dem Bildbeschrieb vor Ort, aus dem Italienischen)*

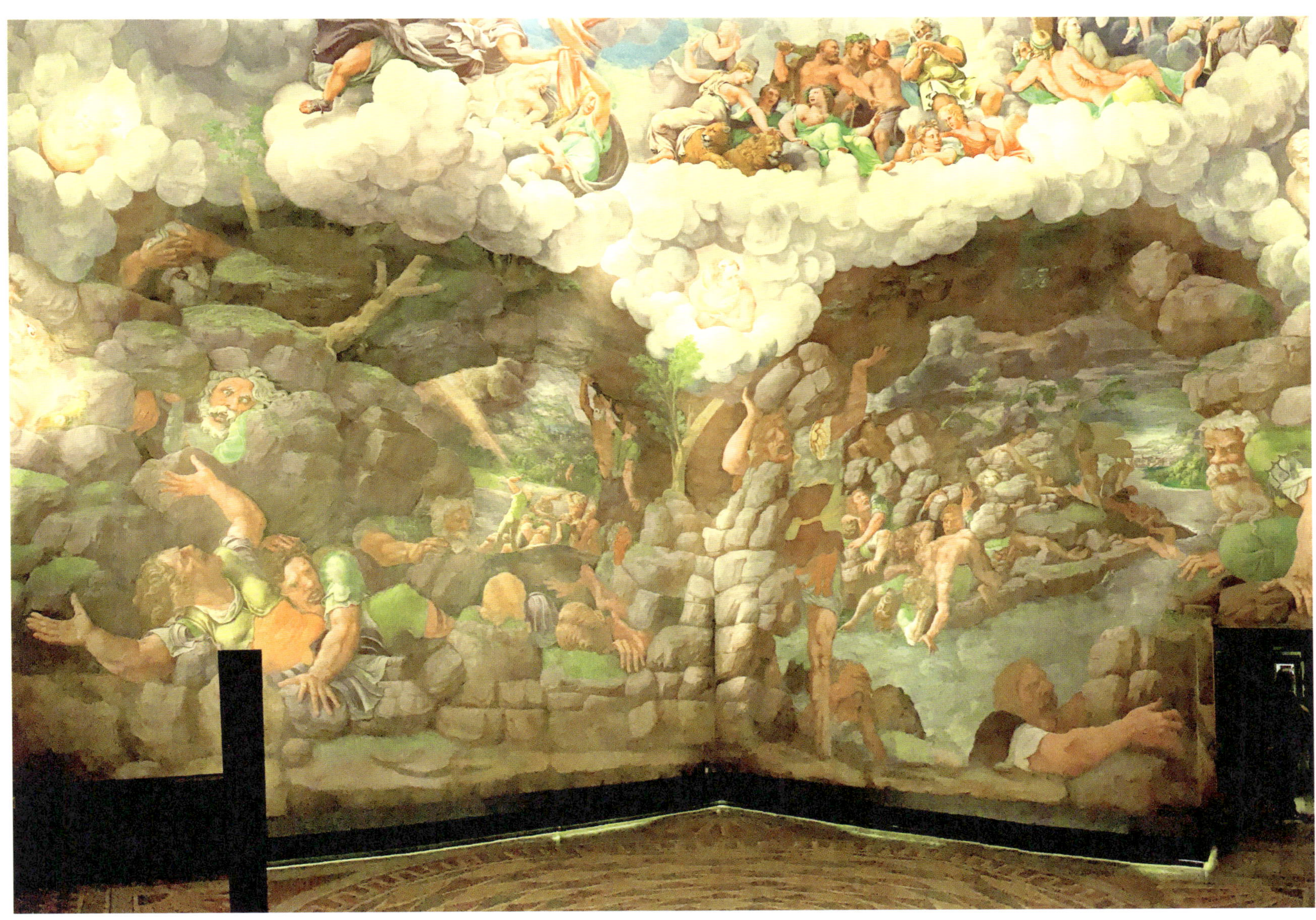

Palazzo Te, Mantua: Raum „Fall der Giganten" (zwischen 1532 und 1535), Komposition von Giulio Romano. Der Mosaikboden stammt aus dem 18. Jh., die Beleuchtung aus dem 20. Jh.

Palazzo Te, Mantua: Room "Fall of the Giants" (between 1532 and 1535), composition by Giulio Romano. The mosaic floor was installed during the 18th century, the lighting in the 20th century.

# TECHNIQUE

A pioneer of panoramic photography was the Frenchman
Frédéric Martens (1806). In 1844, he patented a
clockwork-powered camera that could produce a 150°
panoramic image on a curved metal plate. A famous
example is the wide-angle image "La Seine, la rive gauche
et l'Île de la Cité", a so-called daguerreotype, created in
1846.
The breakthrough of adapting normal perspective
images into a cylindrical projection was achieved in 1995
(Apple Computers: Quicktime VR Authoring Tool Suite;
The Panorama Phenomenon). Today, a wide variety of
stitching and image processing software is available for
creating panoramas and similar designs. This allows the
creation of panoramic images without distortions, parallax
errors, vignetting or color fringes.
The technical possibilities continue to evolve at a
breathtaking pace. Not only is the work to create a
cylindrical projection of a classic panoramic image
much simpler nowadays, but also new kinds of spherical
representations (spherical projections) can be created
(e.g. stereographic projection, "Little Planets images").
Smartphone manufacturers and app developers strive to
serve the ever-growing needs of amateur and professional
photographers for new imaging possibilities.
While circular images tended to lose their importance over
time, panoramic imaging has been further developed and
perfected by both photography enthusiasts and innovative
artists.

# TECHNIK





*Ein Pionier der Panoramaphotographie war der Franzose
Frédéric Martens (1806). Er liess 1844 eine Uhrwerk-be-
triebene Kamera patentieren, die auf einer gebogenen
Metallplatte ein 150°-Panoramabild erzeugen konnte.
Bekannt ist das 1846 geschaffene Weitwinkelbild „La
Seine, la rive gauche et l'Île de la Cité", eine sog.
Daguerreotypie.
Den Durchbruch für die Anpassung von normalperspekti-
vischen Bildern in eine zylindrische Projektion gelang 1995
(Apple Computers: Quicktime VR Authoring Tool Suite;
The Panorama Phenomenon). Für Panoramen und ähn-
liche Bildgestaltungen steht heute eine grosse Vielfalt an
Programmen zum Zusammensetzen (Stitching; engl. von
to stitch: zusammenheften) und Nachbearbeiten zur Verfü-
gung. Damit können mühelos Panoramabilder erzeugt
werden, welche keine störenden Verzerrungen, Parallaxen-
fehler, Vignettierungen oder Farbsäume mehr aufweisen.
Das technisch Mögliche entwickelt sich laufend und in
atemberaubendem Tempo weiter.
Dabei ist nicht nur die Handhabung extrem vereinfacht,
über das Erzeugen eines klassischen Panoramabildes
in zylindrischer Projektion hinaus sind auch kugelförmige
Darstellungen (sphärische Projektion) sowie weitere Spe-
zialmöglichkeiten realisierbar (z. B. stereographische Projektion, „Little Planets"-Bilder). Smartphonehersteller und
App-Entwickler bedienen damit die ungebremste Lust von
Amateuren und Photographen auf neue Abbildungsmöglich-
keiten. Während die Rundgemälde eher an Bedeutung
verloren, wurden Panoramabilder von Photoliebhabern und
innovativen Kunstschaffenden weiterentwickelt und perfek-
tioniert.*

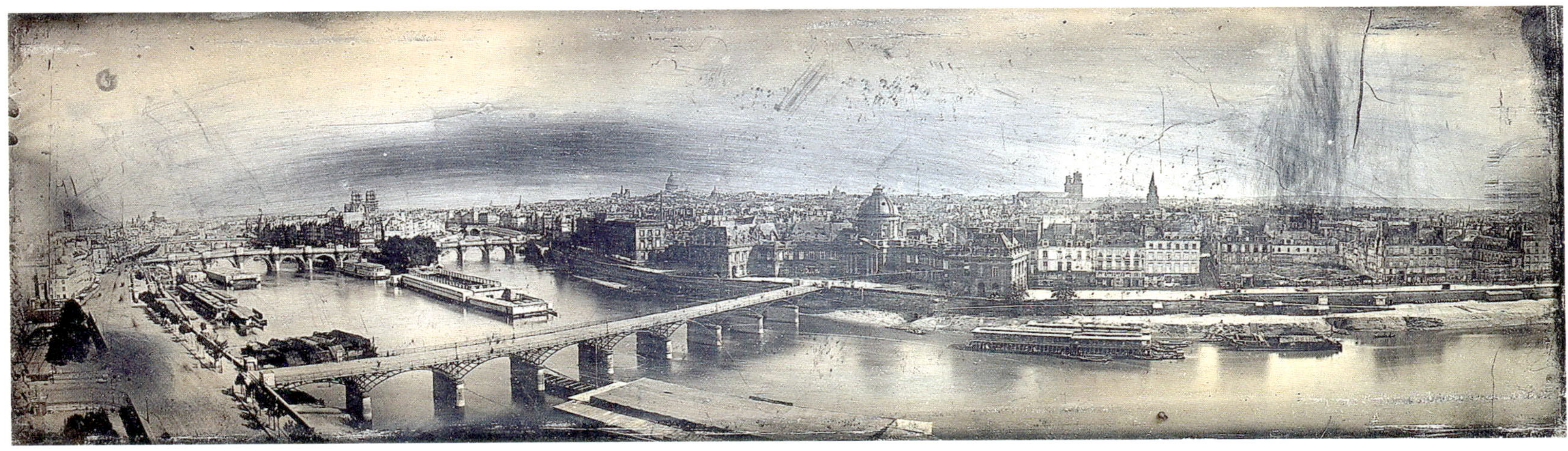

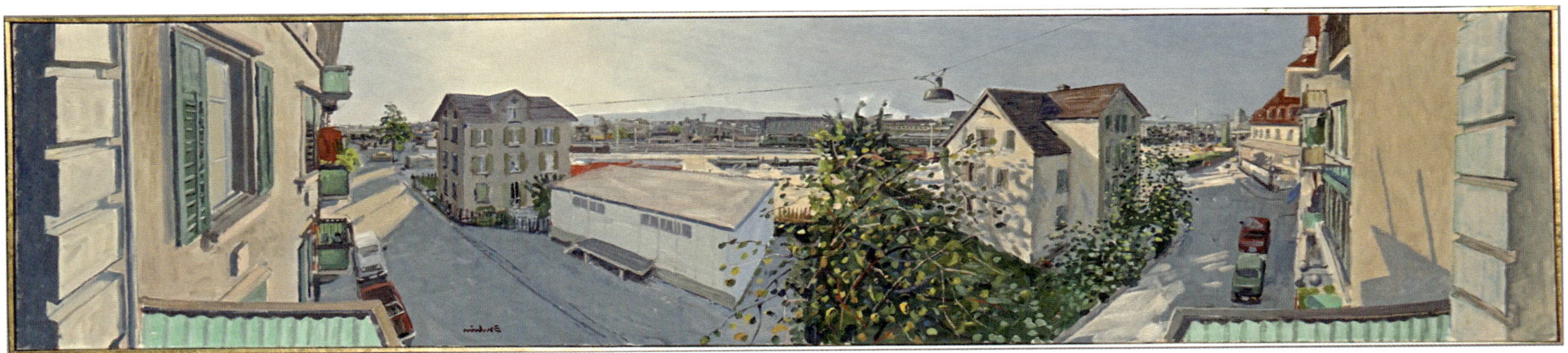

<table>
<tr><td>

Frédéric Martens: (oben) Weitwinkelbild „La Seine, la rive gauche et l'Île de la Cité" (Daguerreotypie, 1846); (unten) Anton Bruhin (*1948): Panorama Zollstrasse, Zürich (Öl auf Leinwand).

</td><td>

Frédéric Martens: (top) Wide-angle photograph "La Seine, la rive gauche et l'Île de la Cité" (daguerreotype, 1846); (bottom) Anton Bruhin (*1948): Panorama Zollstrasse, Zurich (oil on canvas).

</td></tr>
</table>

15

# FOLDOUT

Martens' clockwork wide-angle camera was followed by devices with oscillating lenses (PANOX, Nobles) and slit-shuttered cameras, which could produce complete 360° panoramas by synchronous rotation of the camera and the film.

A new level of simplification was then brought about by digital technology, which stores the image as data. This data can be edited i.e. the images or their components can be re-assembled and adjusted. Nowadays, a high-quality freehand panoramic image can be created using a common smartphone. Just twenty years ago, a professional photographer would have had to invest considerable time and technical effort to achieve the same result. Naturally, there is a demand for high-end products which go far beyond the possibilities of a smartphone. For example, niche products like large-format panoramic films such as those shown on a curved large screen at the Museum of Transport in Lucerne, Switzerland (http://www.verkehrshaus.ch/de/filmtheater).

However, these gigantic panorama productions are not unique in pushing the limits of normal formats and perspectives. As long ago as the 12th century, meter-long, almost endless, pictures appeared in Chinese painting with an impressive richness of detail. Viewers could immerse themselves in these pictures and indulge in the illusion of a panoramic view.

The Chinese pictures are an archetypal example of the foldout format which, due to its flexibility, is still widely used today for panoramic images in tourist information materials or for bird's-eye view plans and maps.



# LEPORELLO

*Auf die Martens'sche Uhrwerk-Weitwinkelkamera folgten Geräte mit Schwinglinsen (PANOX, Nobles) und schliesslich auch Schlitzkameras, welche durch synchrone Drehbewegung der Kamera und des Films komplette 360°-Panoramen erzeugen können.*

*Eine neue Stufe der Vereinfachung brachten sodann die digitalen Aufnahmetechniken, welche die Bildinformation als Datei speichern. Als Datensatz lassen diese sich bearbeiten, d. h. die Bilder resp. Bildteile können nachträglich zusammengesetzt und angepasst werden. Heute lässt sich mit einem gängigen Smartphone spontan und freihändig ein Panoramabild in einer Qualität erzeugen, für welche vor 20 Jahren ein Profiphotograph beträchtlichen technischen und zeitlichen Aufwand hätte treiben müssen. Weiterhin existiert selbstverständlich ein lebhafter „high-end"-Bereich, der weit über die Smartphone-Möglichkeiten hinausgeht; beispielsweise für grossformatige Panoramafilme – Nischenprodukte, wie sie z. B. im Verkehrshaus Luzern auf einer gekrümmten Grossleinwand gezeigt werden (http://www.verkehrshaus.ch/de/filmtheater). Die Grenzen der normalen Formate und Perspektiven wurden aber nicht erst mit den gigantischen Panorama-Inszenierungen gesprengt. Schon seit dem 12. Jahrhundert tauchen in der chinesischen Malerei meterlange Bilder auf, „Endlosbilder" mit eindrücklichem Detailreichtum. Auch in diese Bilder können wir als Betrachter versinken und uns der Illusion eines Rundumblicks hingeben.*

*Dies ist quasi eine Urform des Leporellos (Faltprospekt), welches aufgrund seines beliebig breiten Formates gerne für Panoramabilder als Tourismuswerbung oder für Planansichten in der Vogelperspektive genutzt wird. Eine andere, verwandte Trivialanwendung von Panoramabildern sind die Alpenzeiger-Tafeln.*

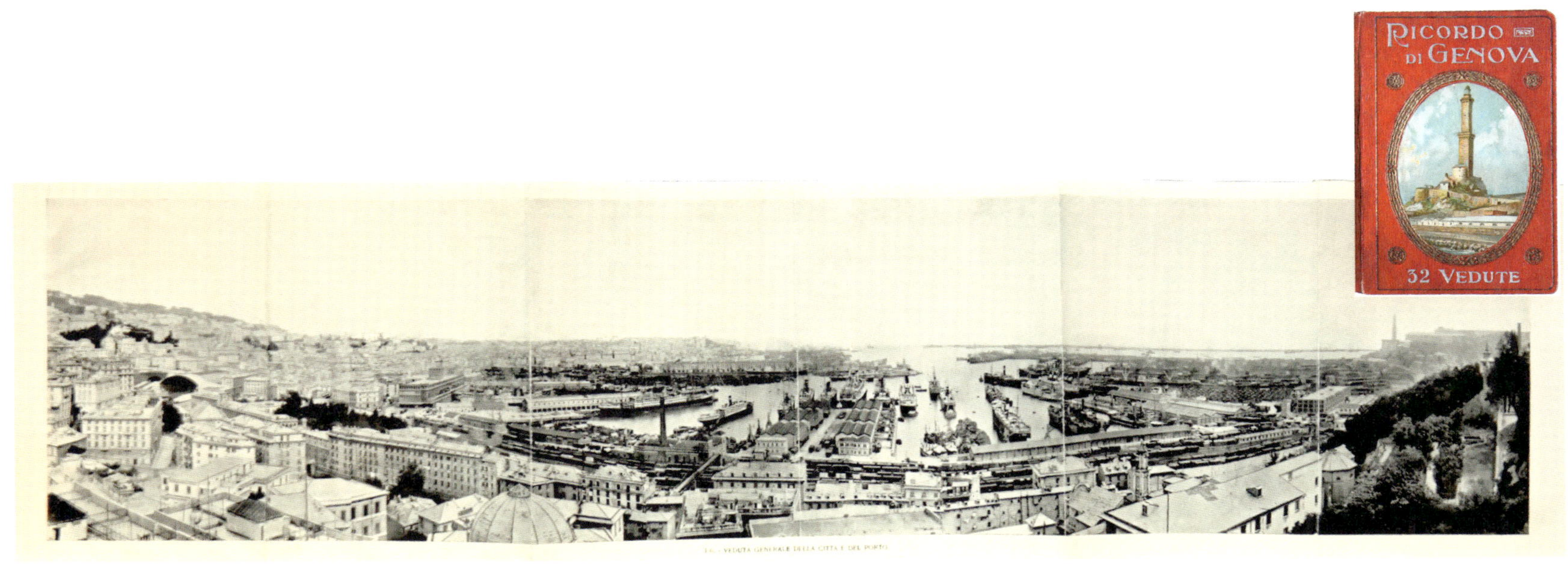

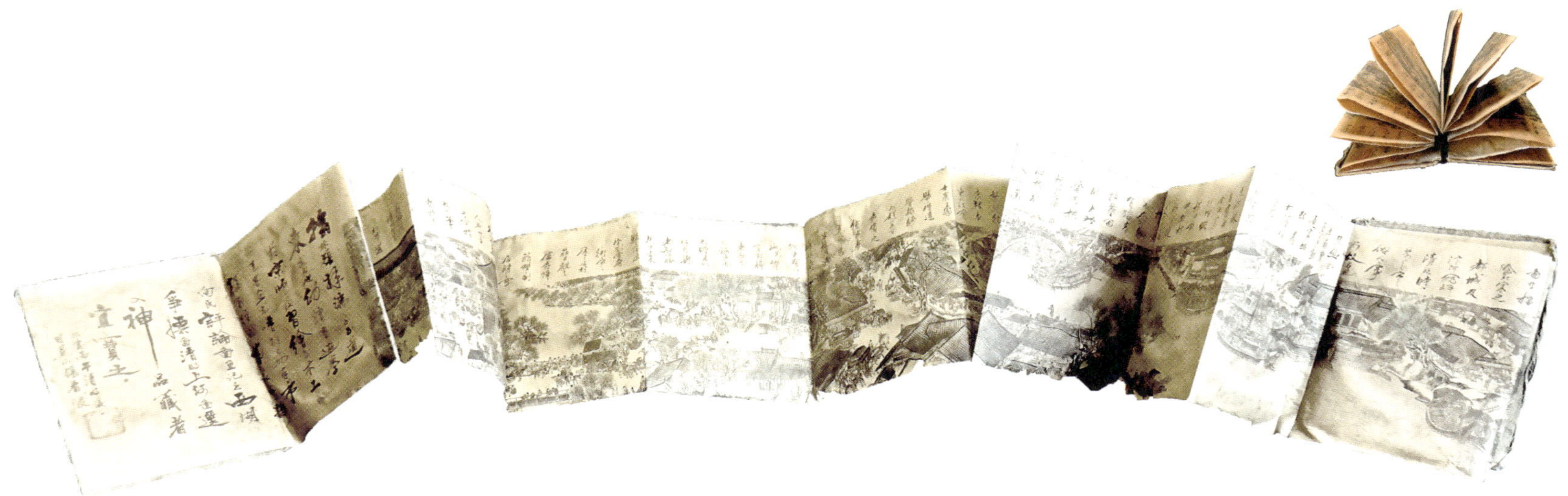

(oben) Historischer Tourismus-Prospekt von Genua, ausklappbares Panorama „Veduta Generale della Città e del Porto", ca. 1920; (unten) Chinesische Endlosbilder, Reproduktion eines antiken Buches.

(top) Historical tourist brochure of Genoa, fold-out panorama "Veduta Generale della Città e del Porto", ca. 1920; (bottom) Chinese endless images, reproduction of an ancient book canvas.

# PERSPECTIVE

What is fascinating about this panoramic imaging technique is its characteristic spatial effect, which is capable of exerting a kind of pull on the viewer – it is surprising how straight lines are transposed into gentle curves, thus distorting the usual structural perspective.

Perspective (from the Latin perspicere, to look through) is the art of representing lines in a picture in such a way that their inclinations and foreshortenings create a plausible impression of space, separated into foreground, middle ground, and background.
Perspective was already in use in ancient times.
During the Renaissance, interest in perspective was rekindled – amongst other reasons due to experiments with the camera obscura.
The architect Filippo Bruneleschi (Florence, 1376) is the pioneer credited with mathematically and geometrically describing and defining the central perspective, based on Euclid's optical theory.
As a technical aid, the "cutting off" technique was developed, as shown in the picture on the right: the draughtman sits next to a wire grid, takes measurements with a compass and transfers this to a sketched grid.
In the past fifteen years, the elaborate methods used to produce panoramic photos, involving wide-angle lenses, spherical mirrors or montages, have increasingly been replaced by digital techniques.
The process of taking and editing images has become much simpler due to the advances in software capabilities.



# PERSPEKTIVE



*Faszinierend an der Panorama-Abbildungstechnik ist die charakteristische Raumwirkung, die auf den Betrachter geradezu eine Art Sogwirkung auszuüben vermag – irritierend, überraschend, wie sich Geraden zu sanften Biegungen verzerren und der gewohnte perspektivische Bildaufbau aufgehoben wird.*
*Perspektive (von lateinisch perspicere, hindurchsehen) gilt als die Kunst, Linien in einem Bild so darzustellen, dass durch deren Neigungen und Verkürzungen ein plausibler Raumeindruck entsteht, mit Vorder-, Mittel- und Hintergrund. Ansatzweise wurden perspektivische Darstellungen schon im Altertum genutzt.*
*In der Renaissance wurde die Perspektive quasi wiederentdeckt – auch aufgrund der Experimente mit der Camera obscura.*
*Als Pionier gilt der Baumeister und Architekt Filippo Bruneleschi (Florenz, 1376) der, ausgehend von Euklids optischer Lehre, die Zentralperspektive mathematisch und geometrisch exakt beschrieb und definierte.*
*Als technische Hilfe wurde das „Abschnüren" entwickelt, wie es im Bild rechts dargestellt ist: Der Zeichner sitzt neben einem Drahtgitter, nimmt mit dem Zirkel Mass und überträgt dies ins Raster seiner Skizze.*
*In den letzten 15 Jahren wurden die aufwändigen photographischen Panoramatechniken mit Extremweitwinkelobjektiven, sphärischen Spiegeln oder Montagetechniken zunehmend von digitalen Methoden verdrängt.*
*Vor allem vereinfachte sich die nachträgliche Montage und Entzerrung von Einzelaufnahmen durch die Bildbearbeitungsprogramme, unterstützt durch Aufnahmesoftware, die das spätere Anpassen und Zusammensetzen (Stitching) auf einfache Weise ermöglichen.*

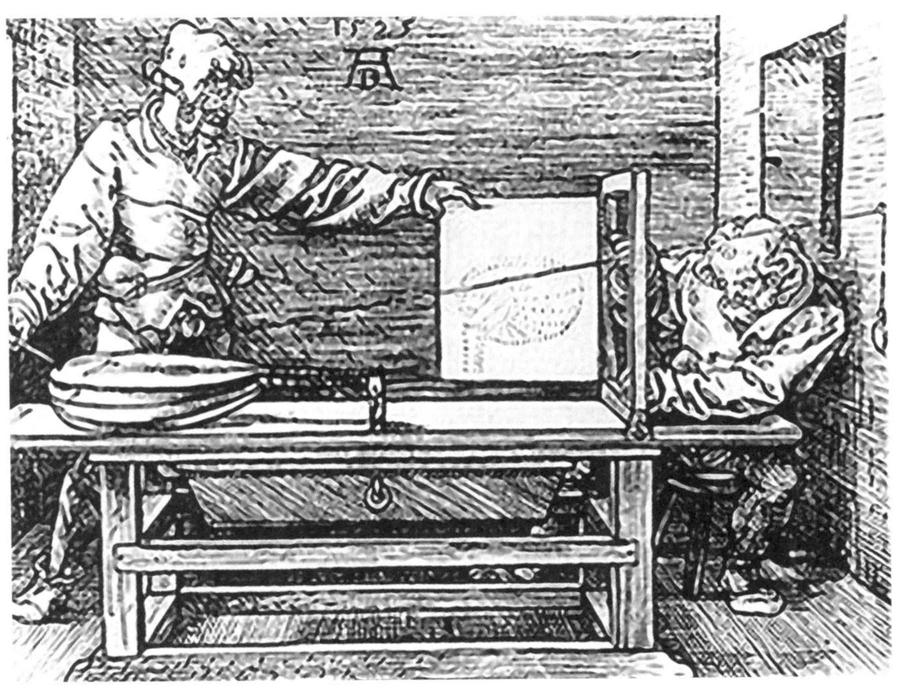

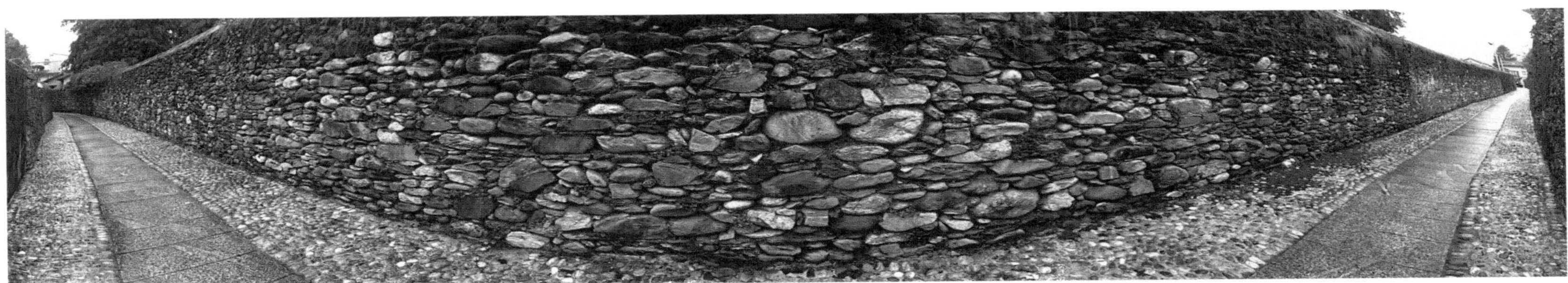

(oben) Aus Albrecht Dürers „Unterweysung der Messung mit dem Zirckel un richtscheyt" (1525); (unten) Gasse in Ascona: Die Panoramaaufnahme erzeugt zwei Fluchtpunkte.

(top) From Albrecht Dürer's "Unterweysung der Messung mit dem Zirckel un richtscheyt" (1525); (bottom) Alley in Ascona: This panorama image creates two vanishing points.

# EXKURSUS

In terms of cultural history, rolling techniques are extremely old. There are cylindrical seals, which were found in archaeological excavations in southern Mesopotamia (Iraq) and have been dated as 5,000 to 6,000 years old. The cylindrical seals, slightly smaller than a bottle cork, are made of stone (or gemstone such as lapis lazuli). They are decoratively carved and their pattern could be transferred by rolling them onto a malleable material, for example clay (cf. image right, above) or sealing wax.

The creation of a cylindrical tool to produce a flat, relief-like printed product was an impressive cultural achievement.

A seal with a rolled depiction produces an image which is unique to the owner and therefore affords a certain level of protection against forgery. Rolling stamps are also used in many arts and crafts techniques, especially for decorating ceramics. An example of another type of handicraft is the small ceramic fruit bowl shown on the facing page. Here, a plaster cast was made from a melon, and this was used as the mold for the ceramic object. A modern-day example is the rolling pin used to produce the "Tirggel" cookie, a regional speciality from Zurich, Switzerland.

In summary, roller techniques have been used in a wide variety of applications in the development of printing technology.

# EXKURS

*Kulturgeschichtlich sind Abrolltechniken sehr alt. Berühmt sind die Rollsiegel oder Siegelzylinder, welche bei archäologischen Grabungen in Südmesopotamien (Irak) gefunden wurden und auf ein Alter von 5000 bis 6000 Jahren datiert sind.*

*Diese Rollsiegel, etwas kleiner als ein Flaschenkorken, bestehen aus Stein (bzw. Edelstein wie Lapislazuli). Sie sind kunstvoll geschnitzt und übertragen ihr Muster beim Abrollen auf ein formbares Material, beispielsweise Ton (vgl. Bild rechts oben) oder Siegelmasse.*

*Das Schaffen eines zylindrischen Werkzeugs zur Erzeugung eines flächigen, reliefartigen Druckprodukts ist jedenfalls eine eindrückliche kulturhistorische Leistung.*

*Ein Siegel mit Abrollbild ist bis zu einem bestimmten Grad unverwechselbar und erlangt dadurch eine gewisse Fälschungssicherheit.*

*Ähnliche Rollstempel werden in vielen kunsthandwerklichen Techniken verwendet, insbesondere zur Verzierung von Keramik. Ein einfaches, analoges Werkzeug in heutiger Zeit ist das Abroll-Wallholz für gewisse Teigprodukte (z. B. das in Zürich verbreitete Feingebäck „Tirggel").*

*Auf die sehr breite Anwendung von Rollen- bzw. Walzentechniken in der Entwicklung der Druckindustrie sei hier nur summarisch verwiesen. Ein kunsthandwerkliches Beispiel ist die gegenüber abgebildete kleine Fruchtschale. Dazu wurde von einer Melone ein Gipsabdruck erstellt, der als Form für die Keramikmasse verwendet wurde.*

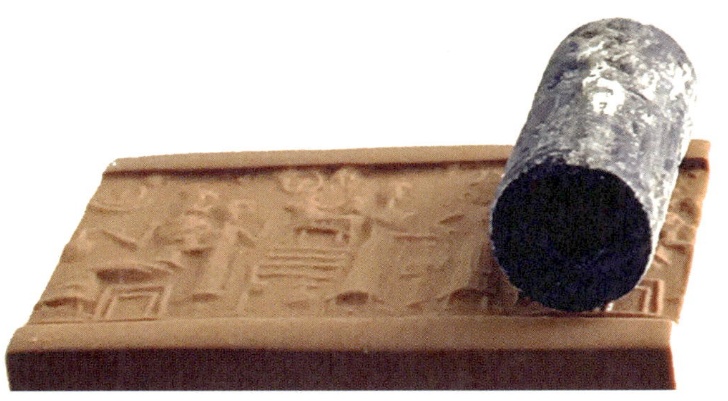

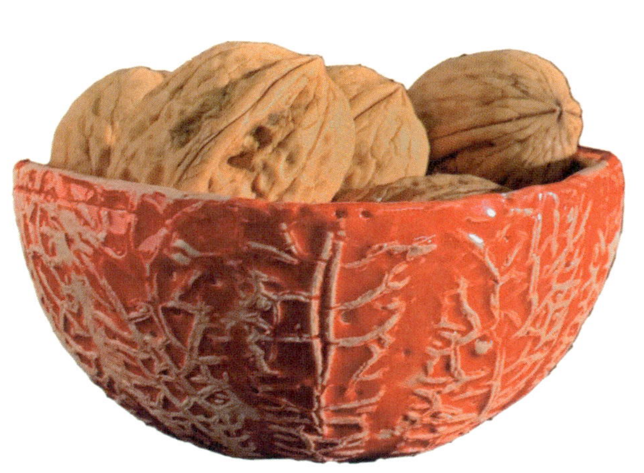

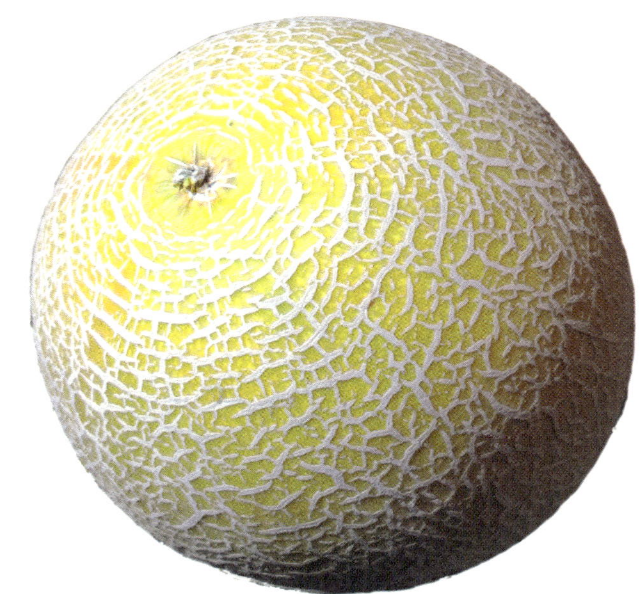

(oben) Rollsiegel, Pergamonmuseum Berlin (vgl. Text).
(links) Fruchtschale aus Keramik; (rechts) Netzmelone mit charakteristischer Oberflächenstruktur (vgl. auch S. 94/95).

(top) Cylindrical seal, Pergamon Museum Berlin (cf. text).
(left) Ceramic fruit bowl; (right) Honeydew melon with its characteristic growth cracks surface structure (cf. also pp. 94/95).

IMAGESTRIP

MAGESTRIPI

AGESTRIPIM

GESTRIPIMA

ESTRIPIMAG

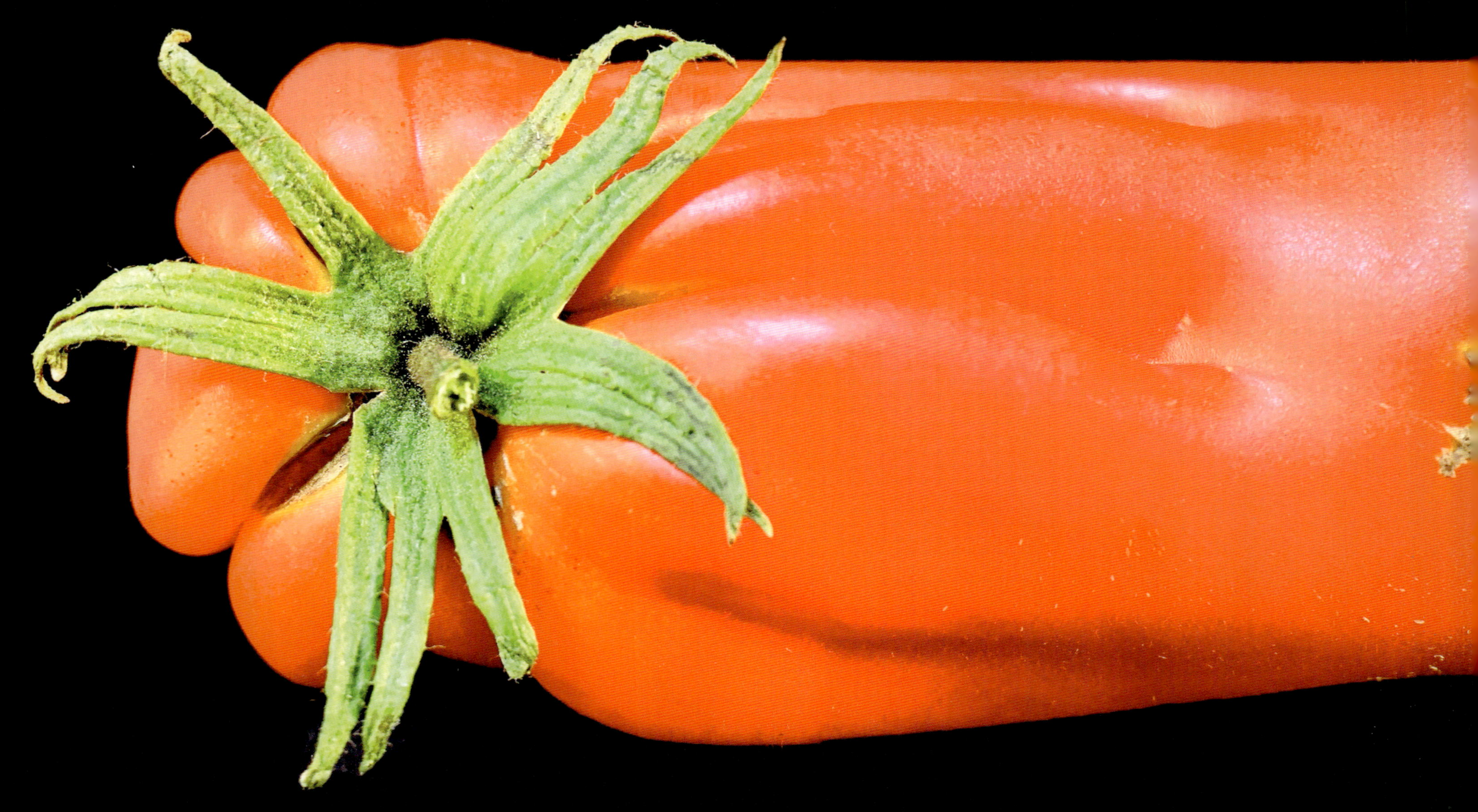

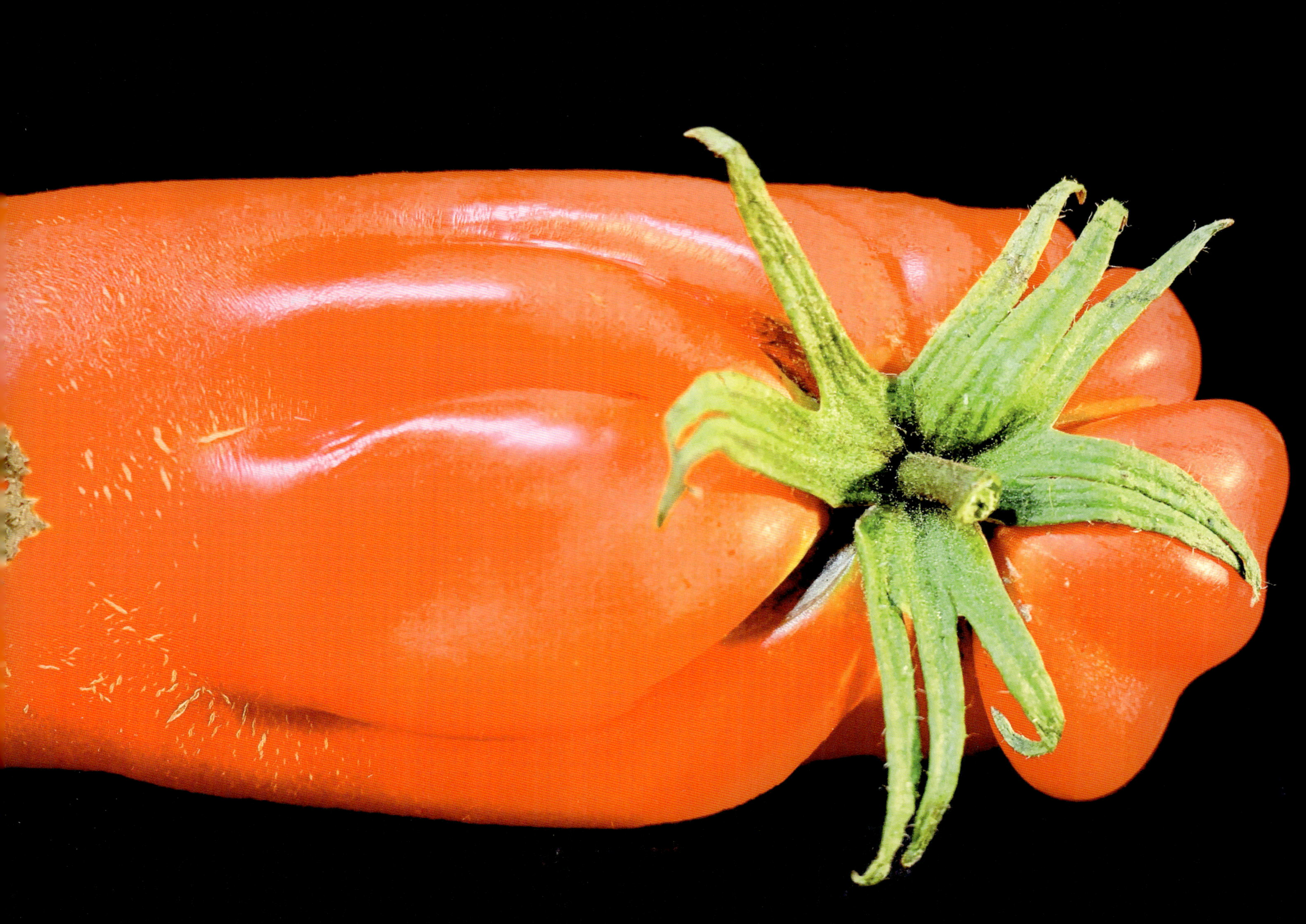

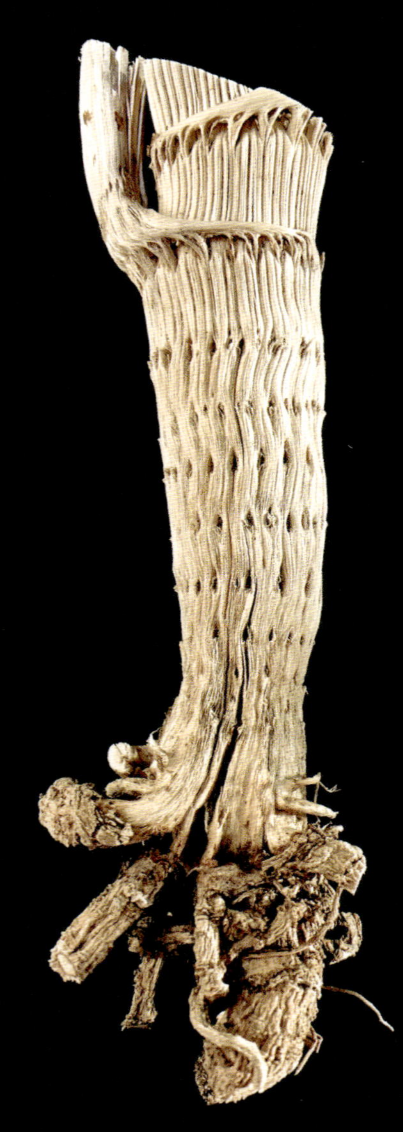

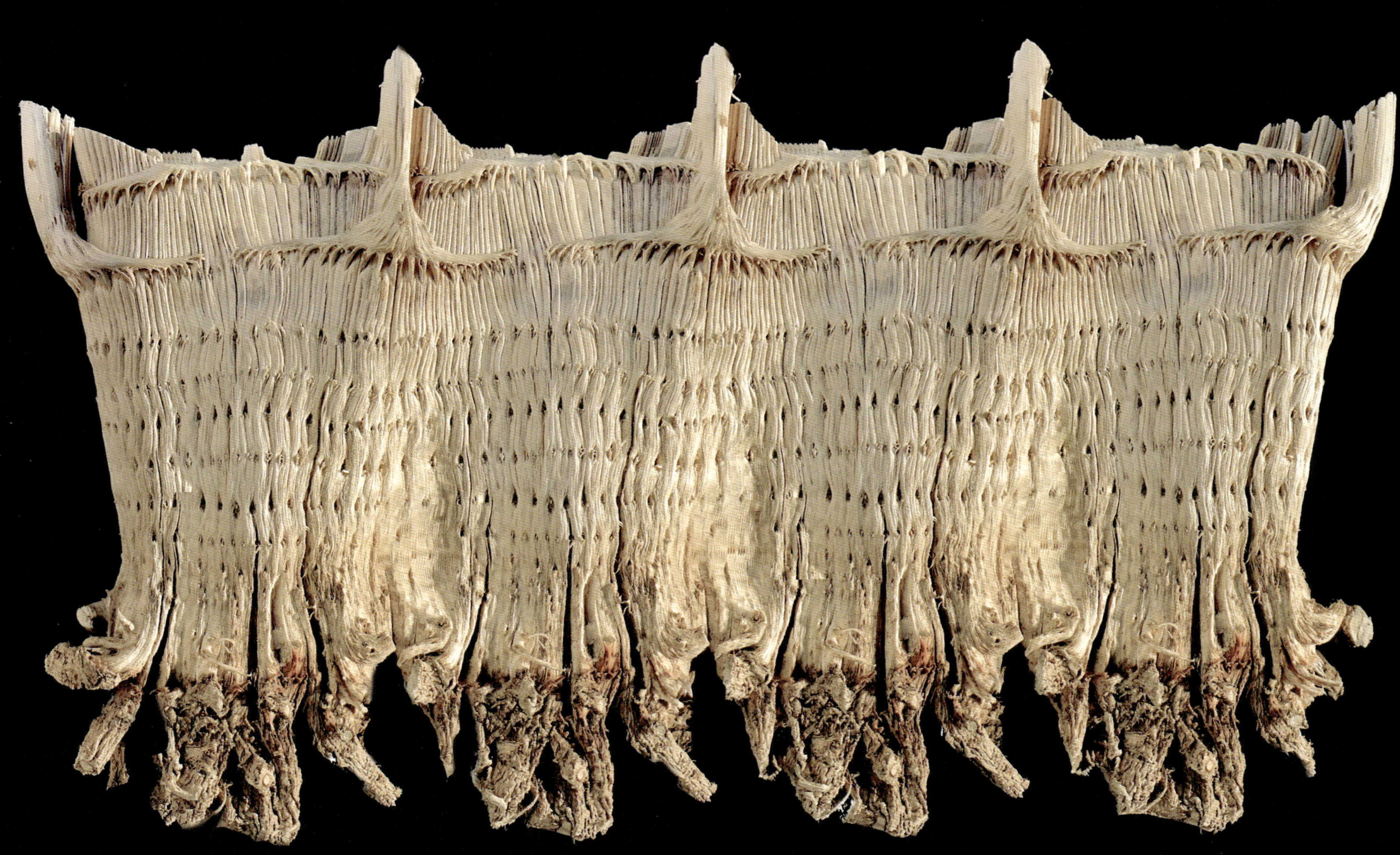

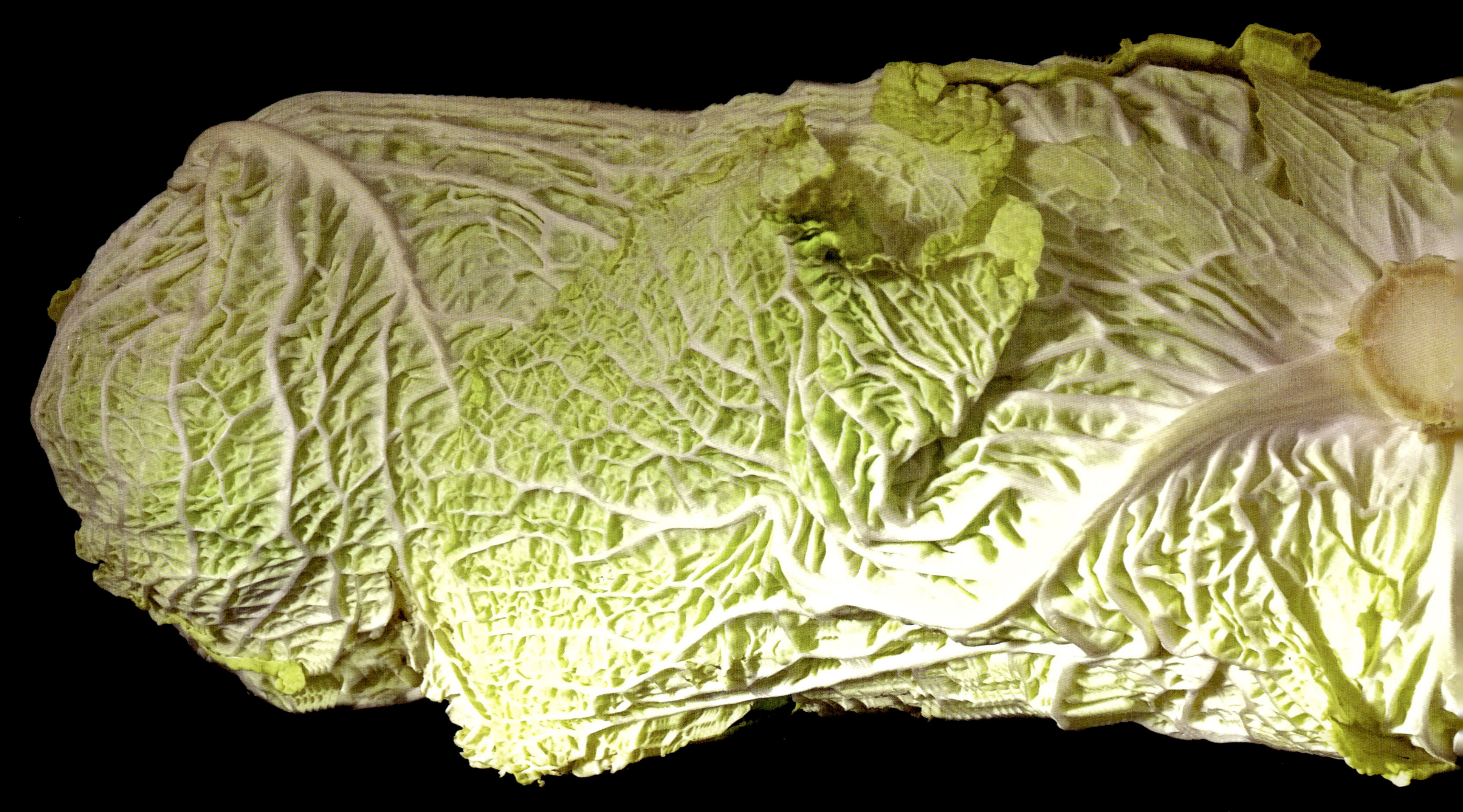

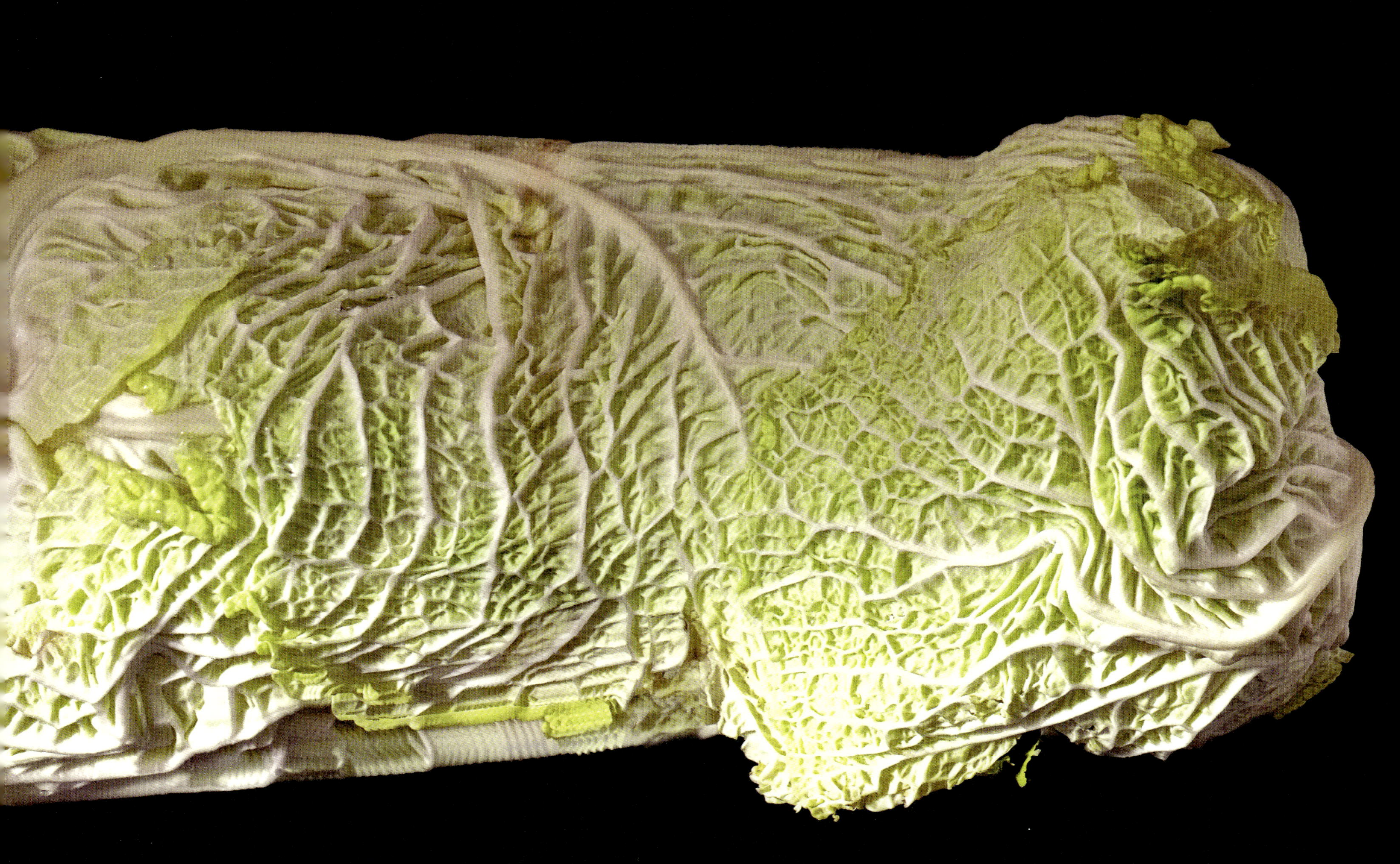

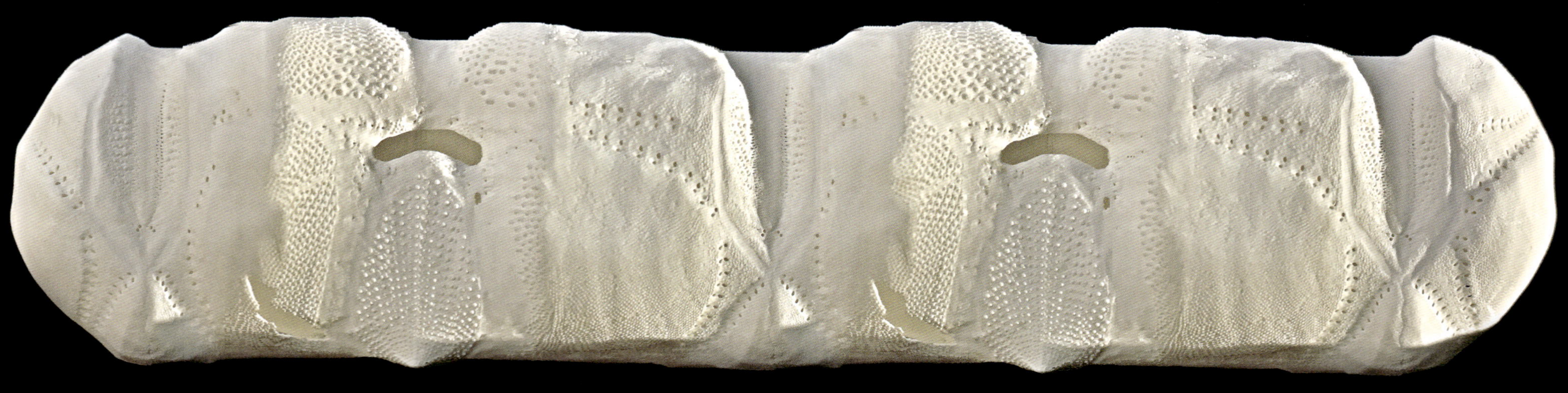

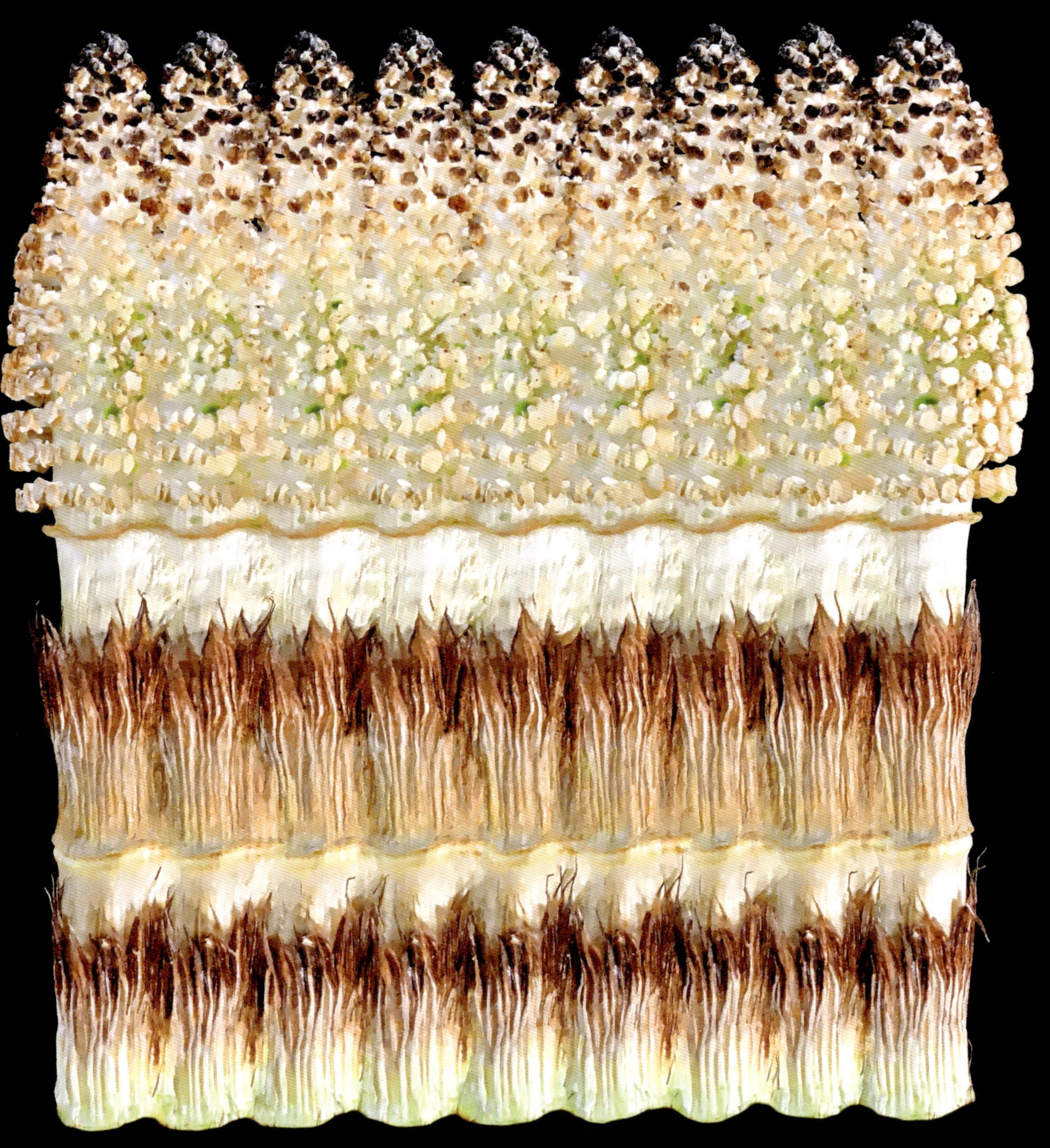

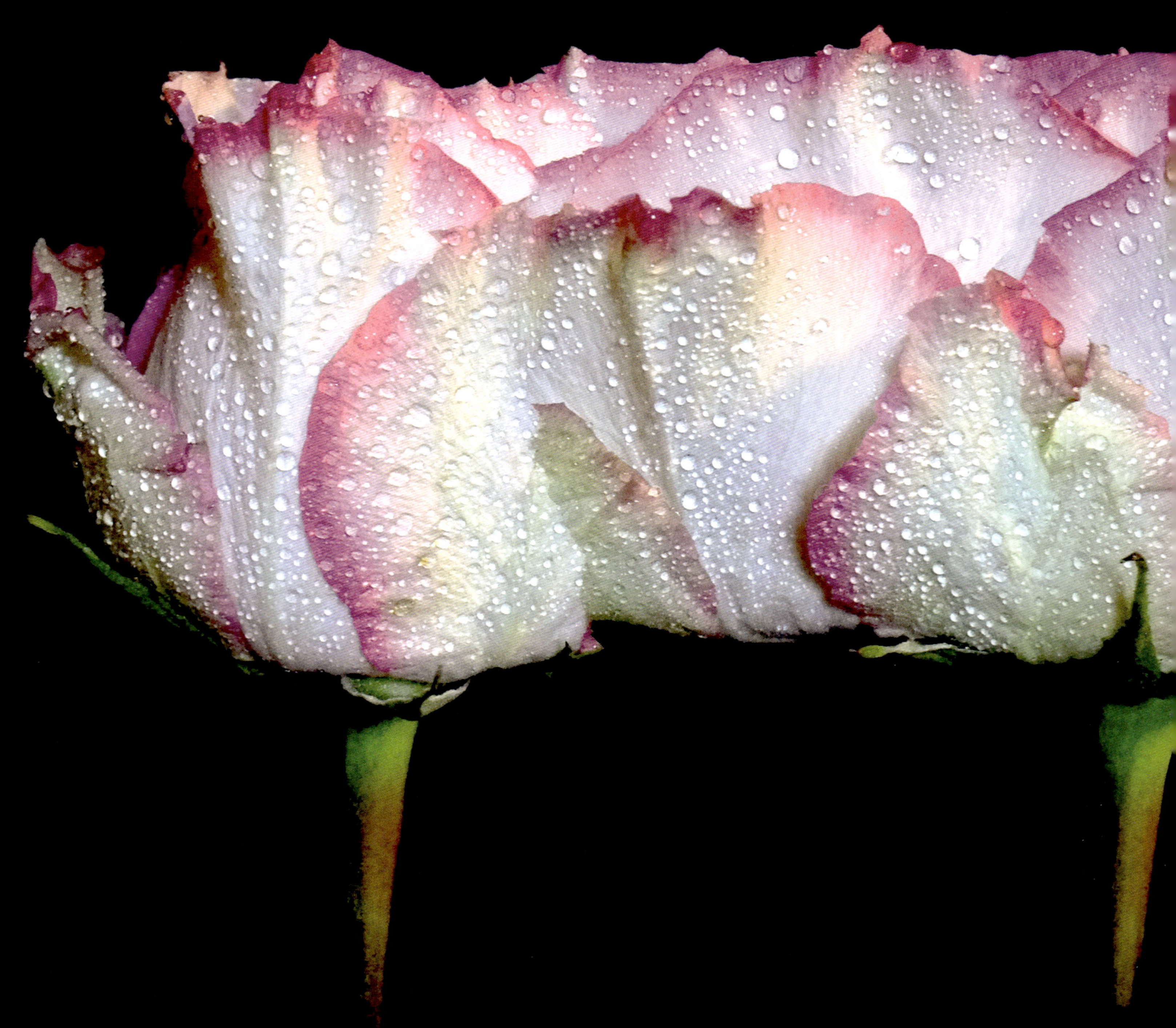

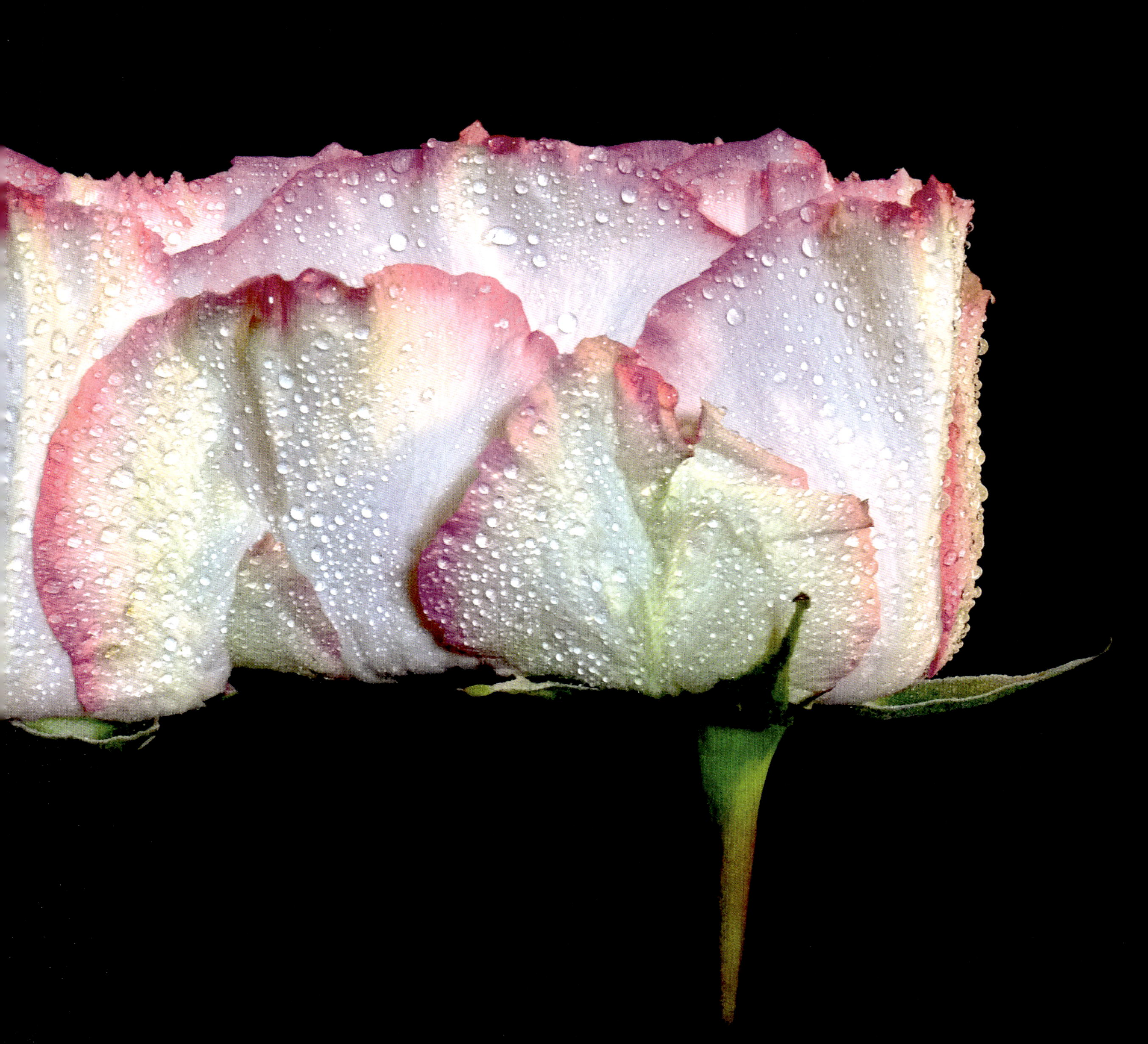

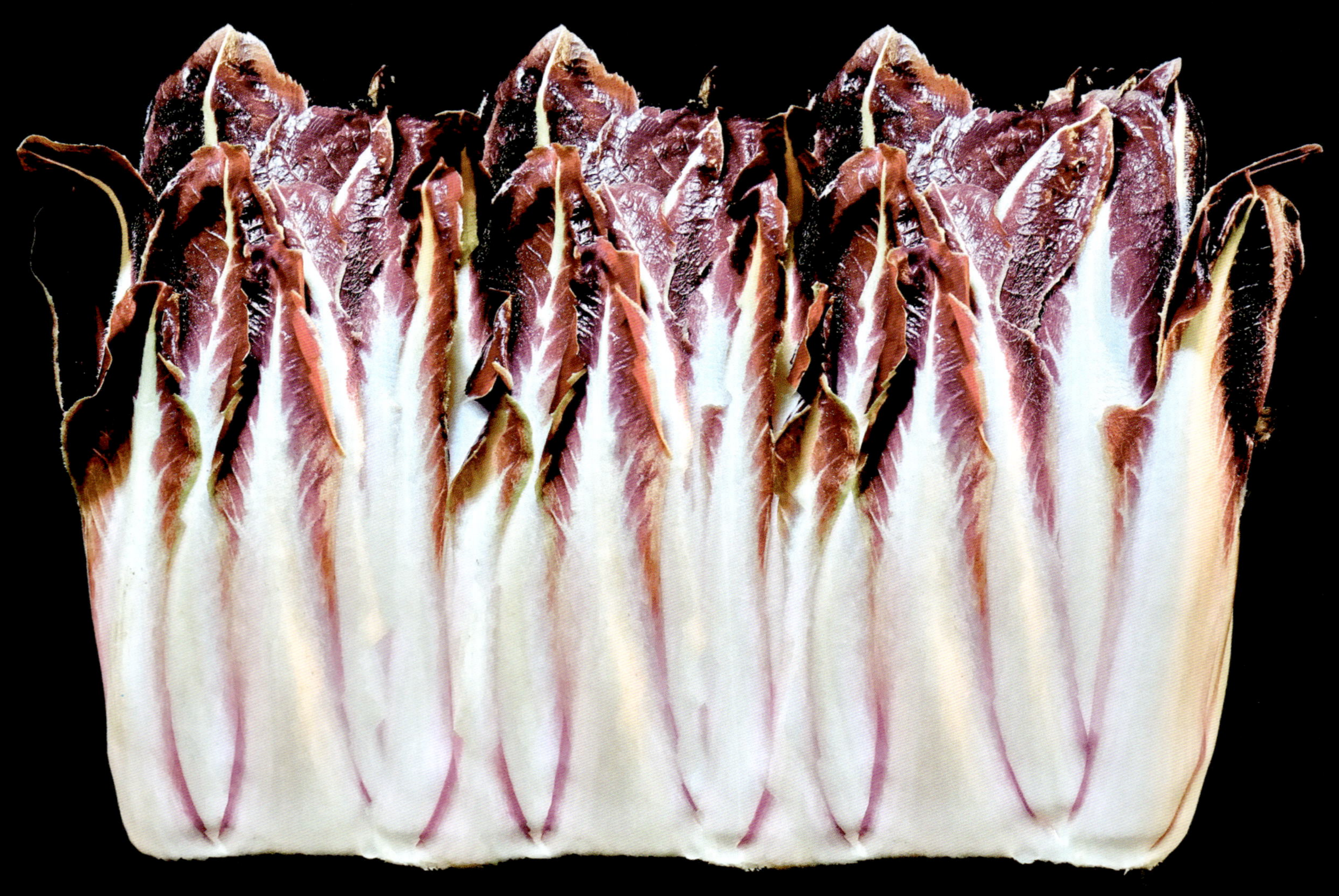

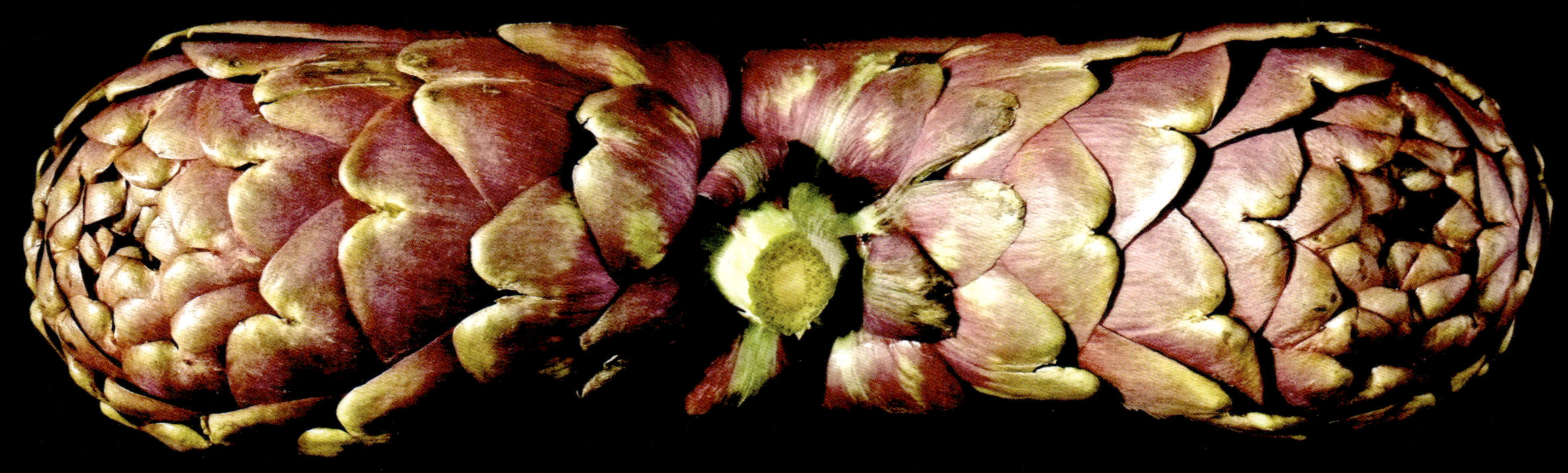

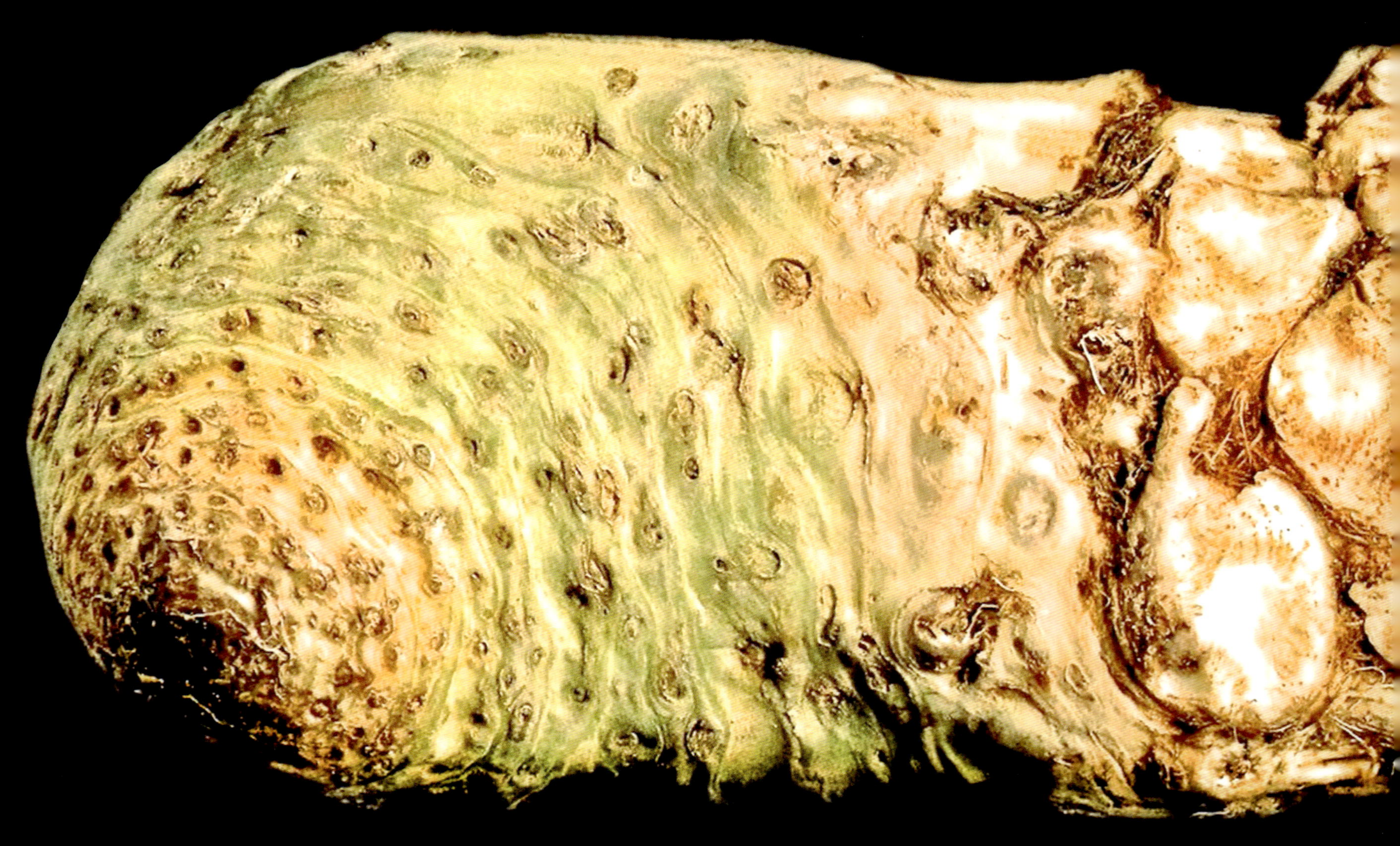

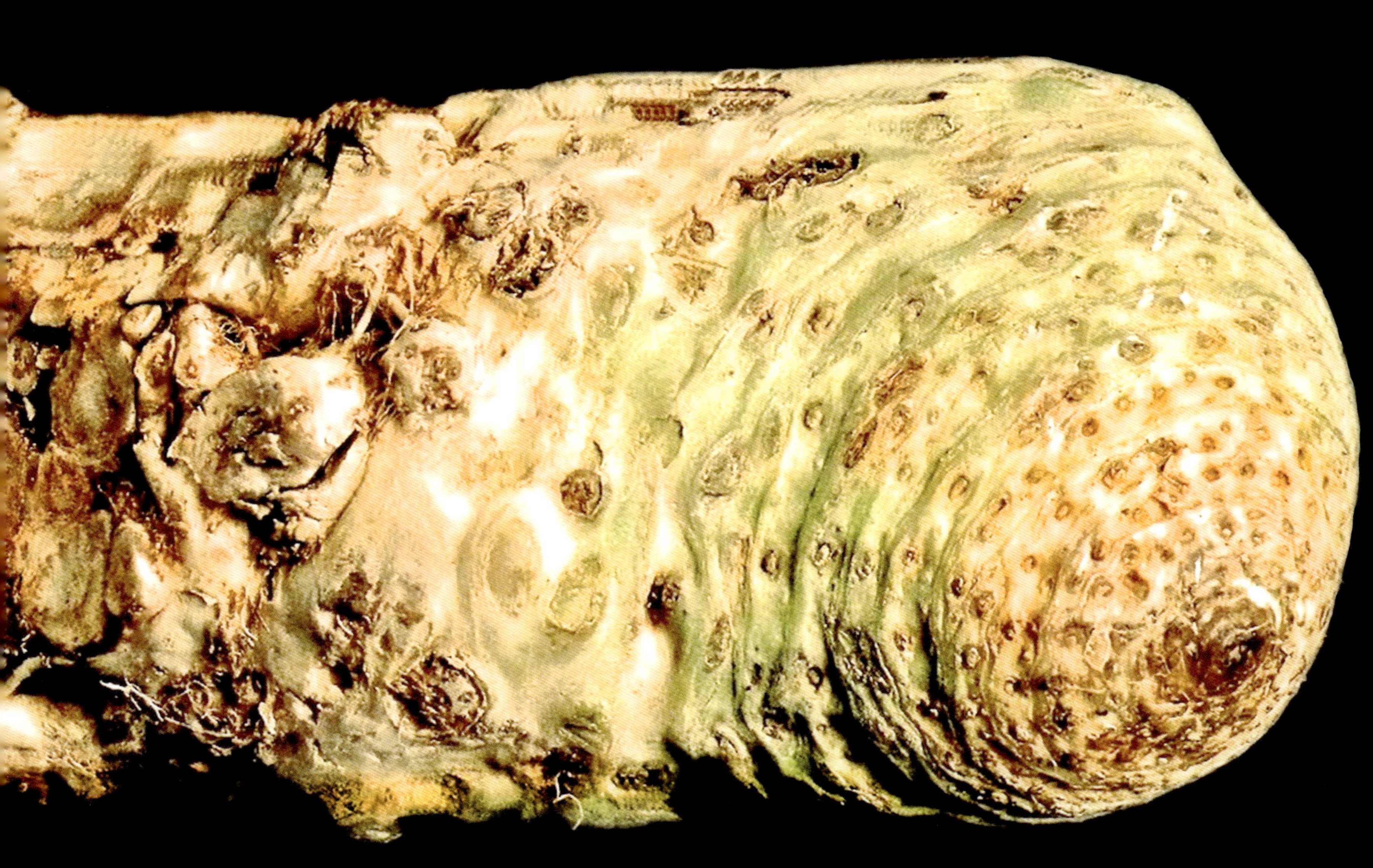

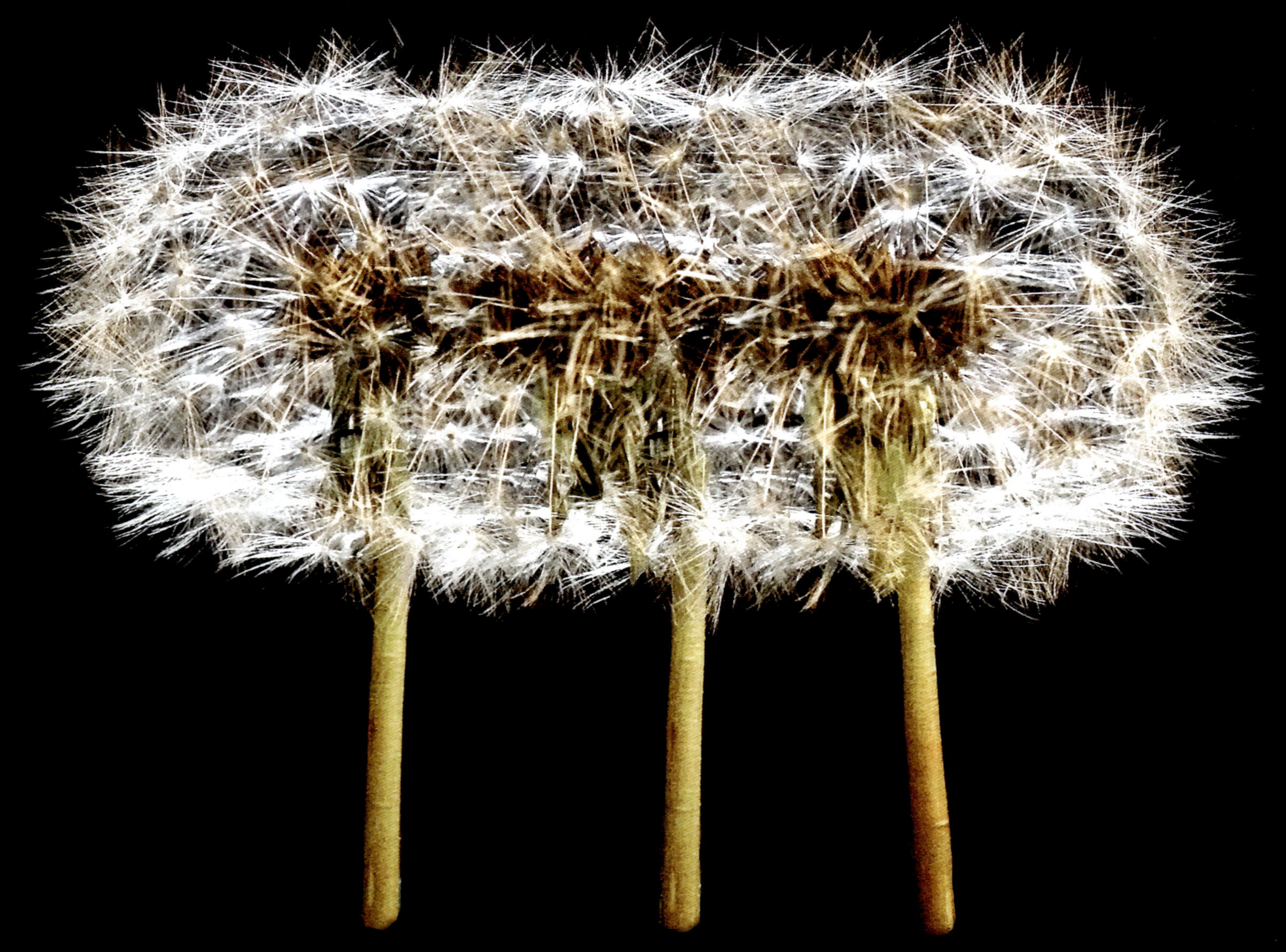

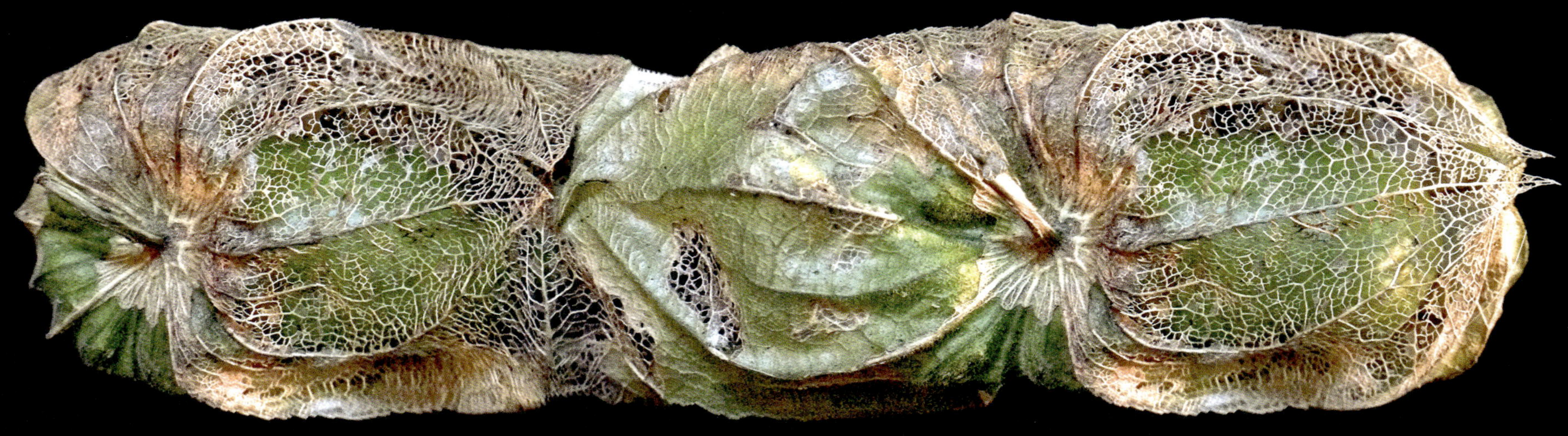

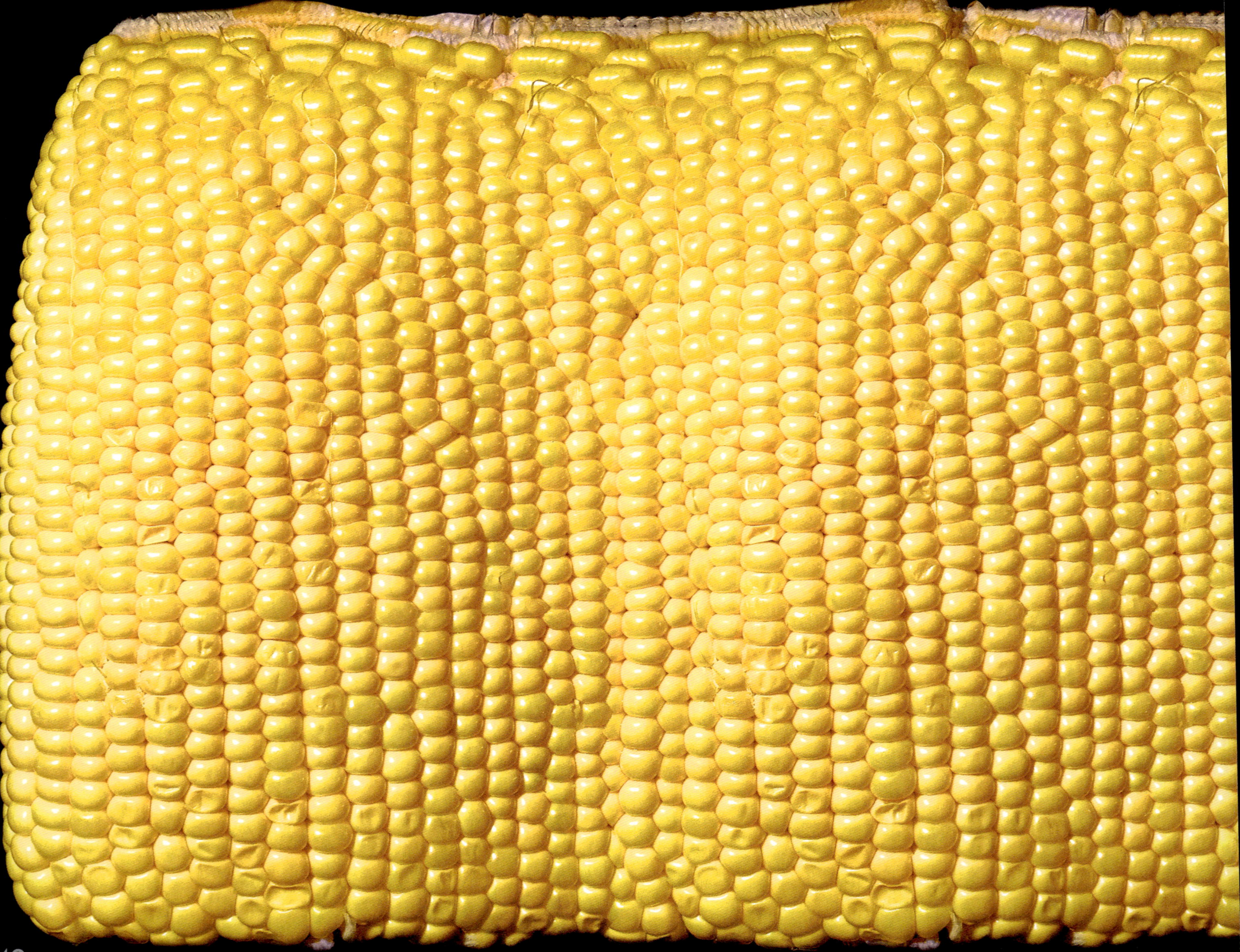

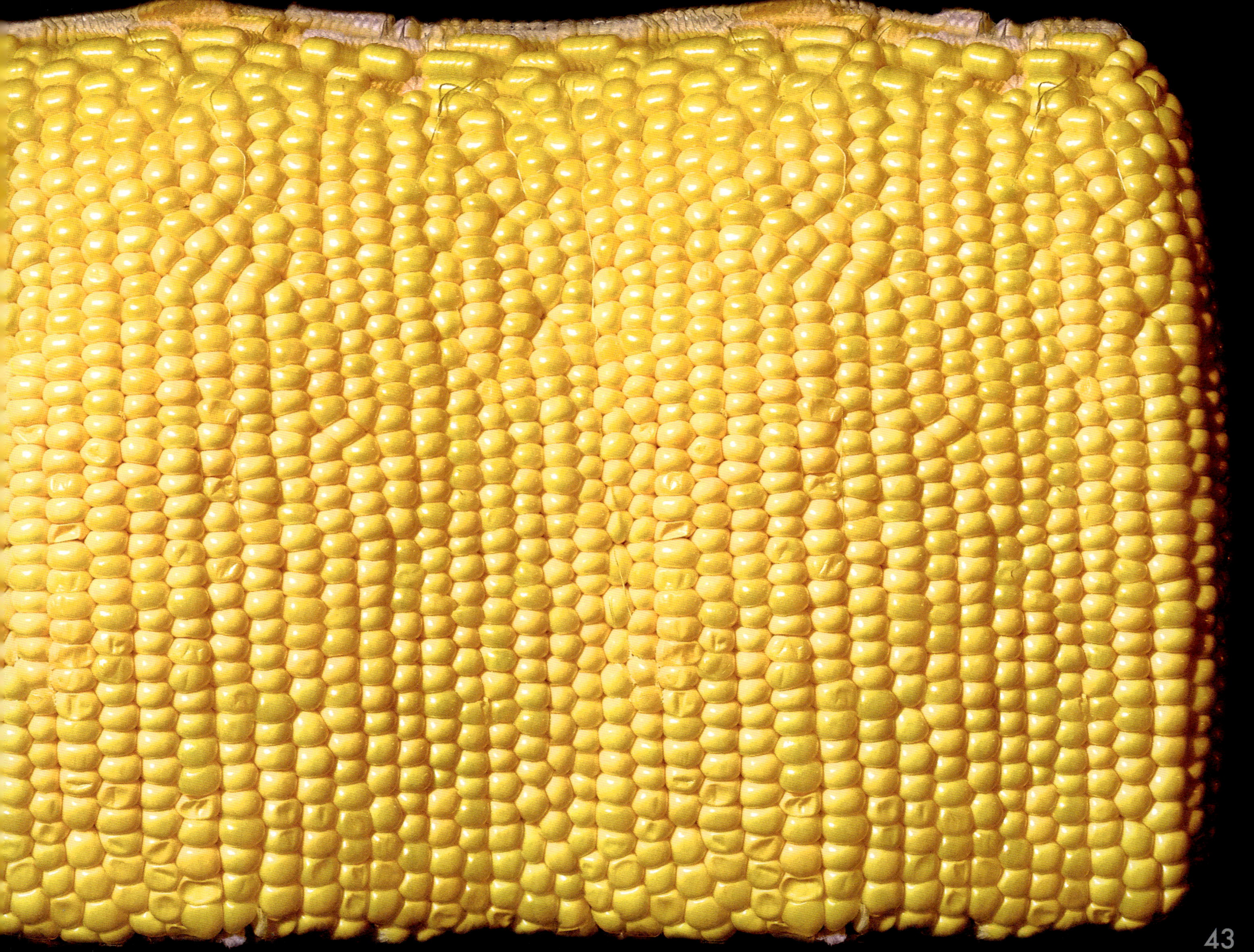

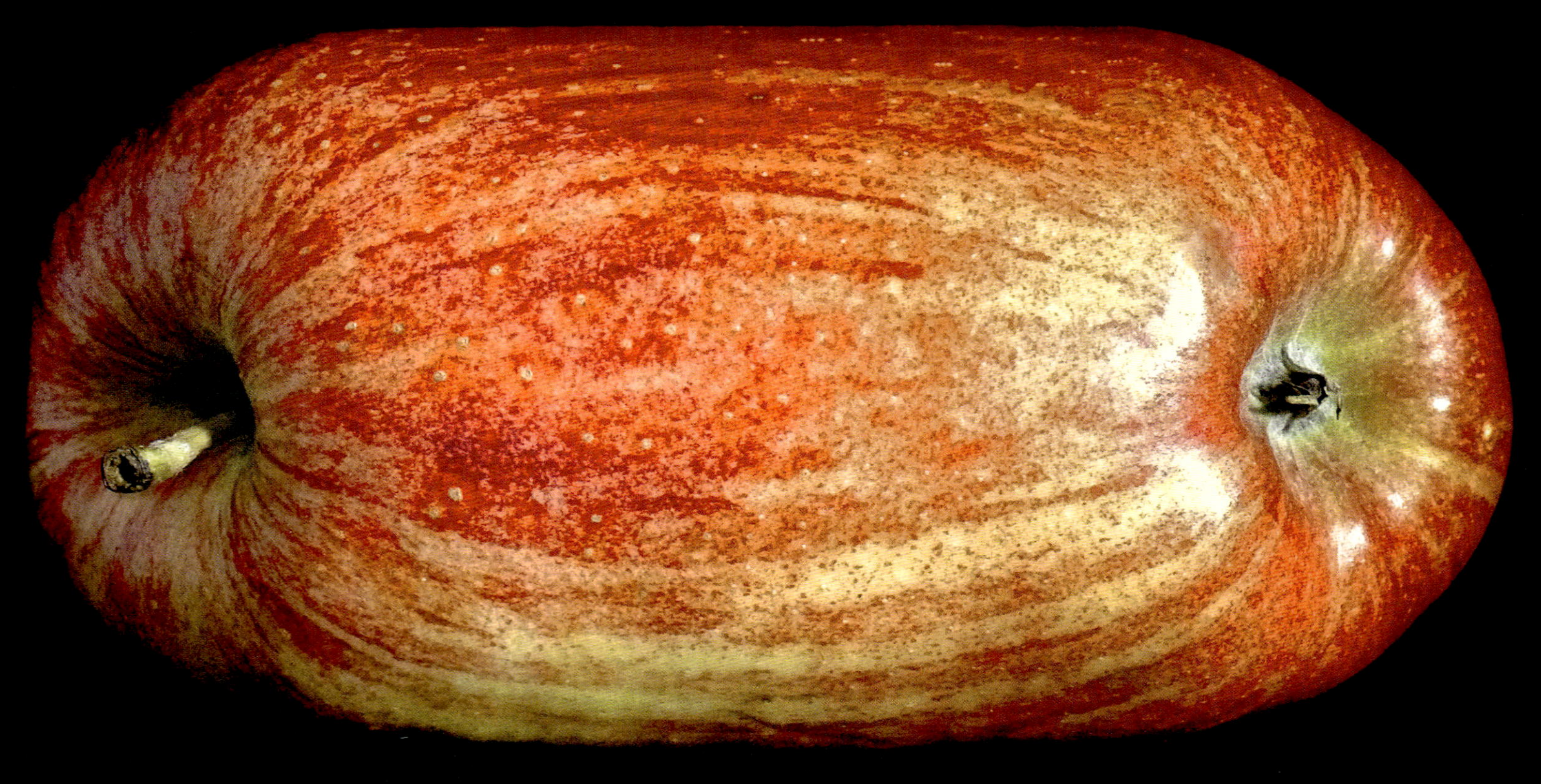

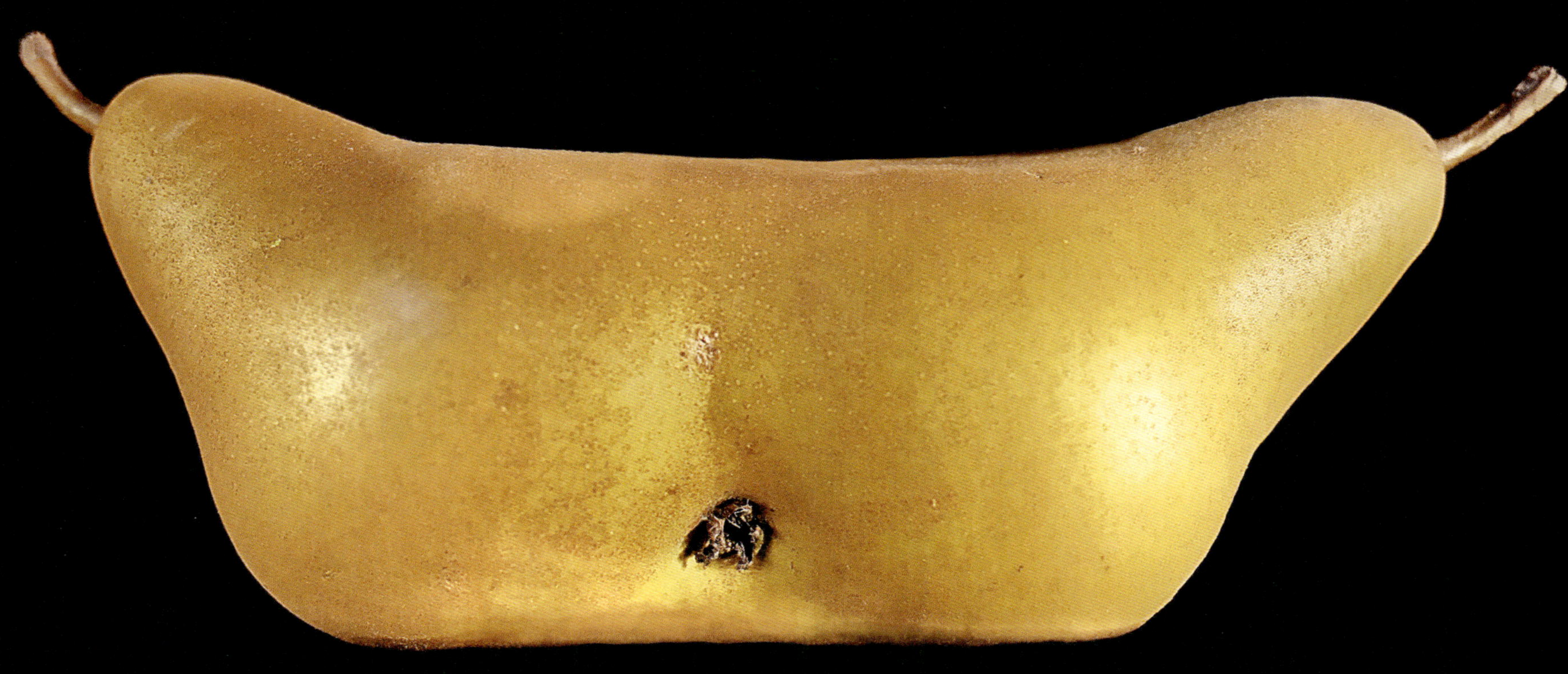

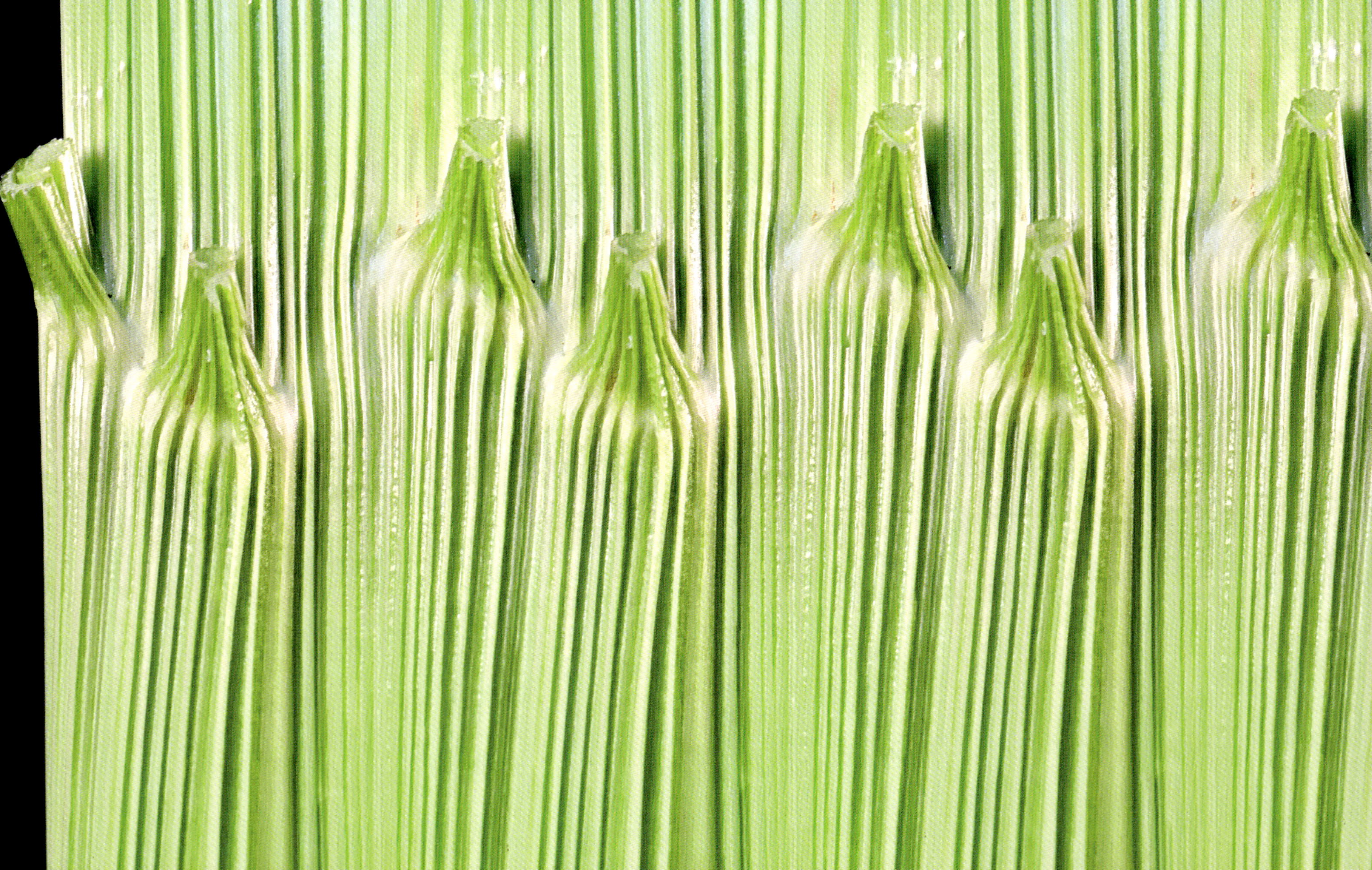

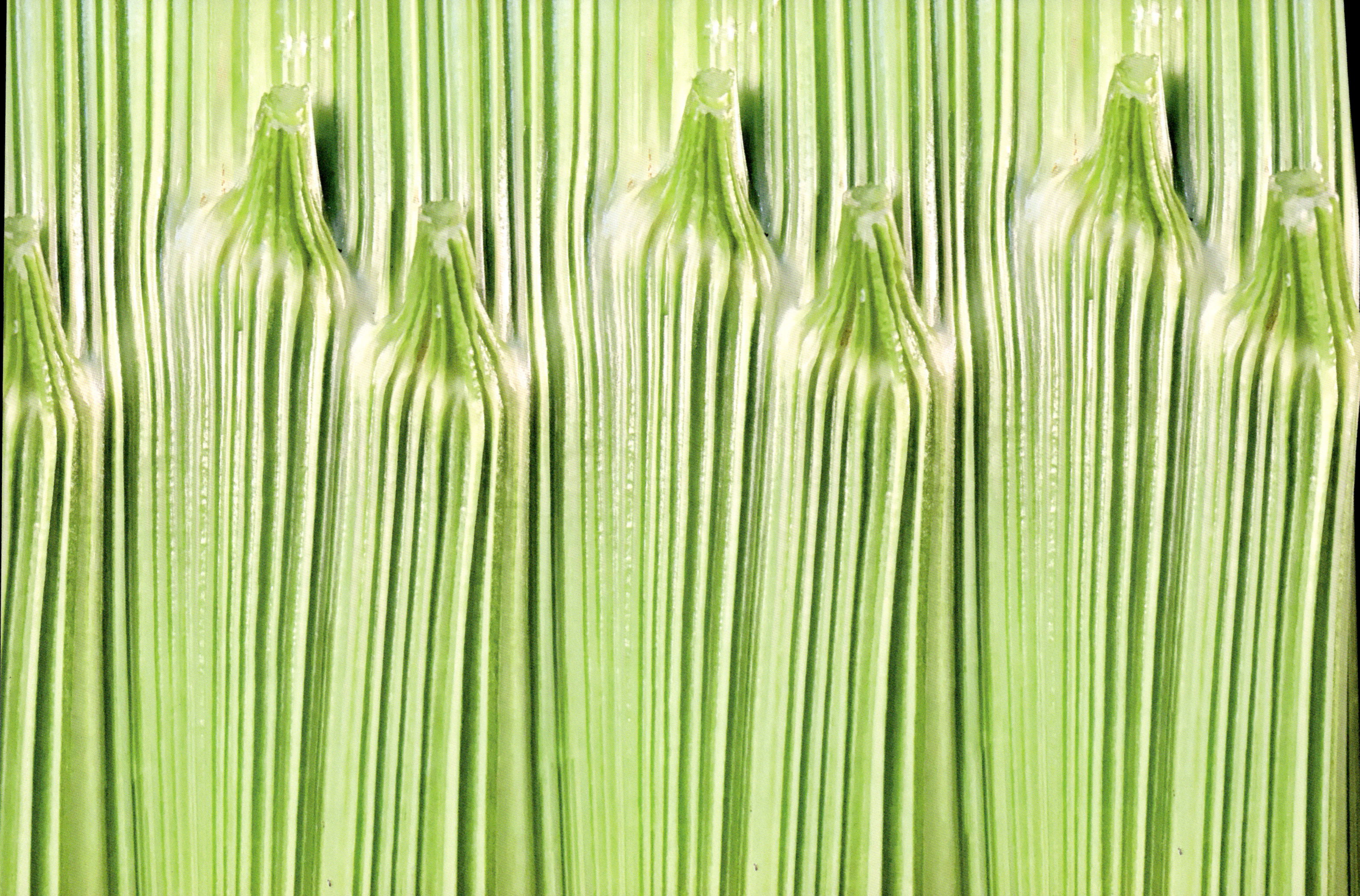

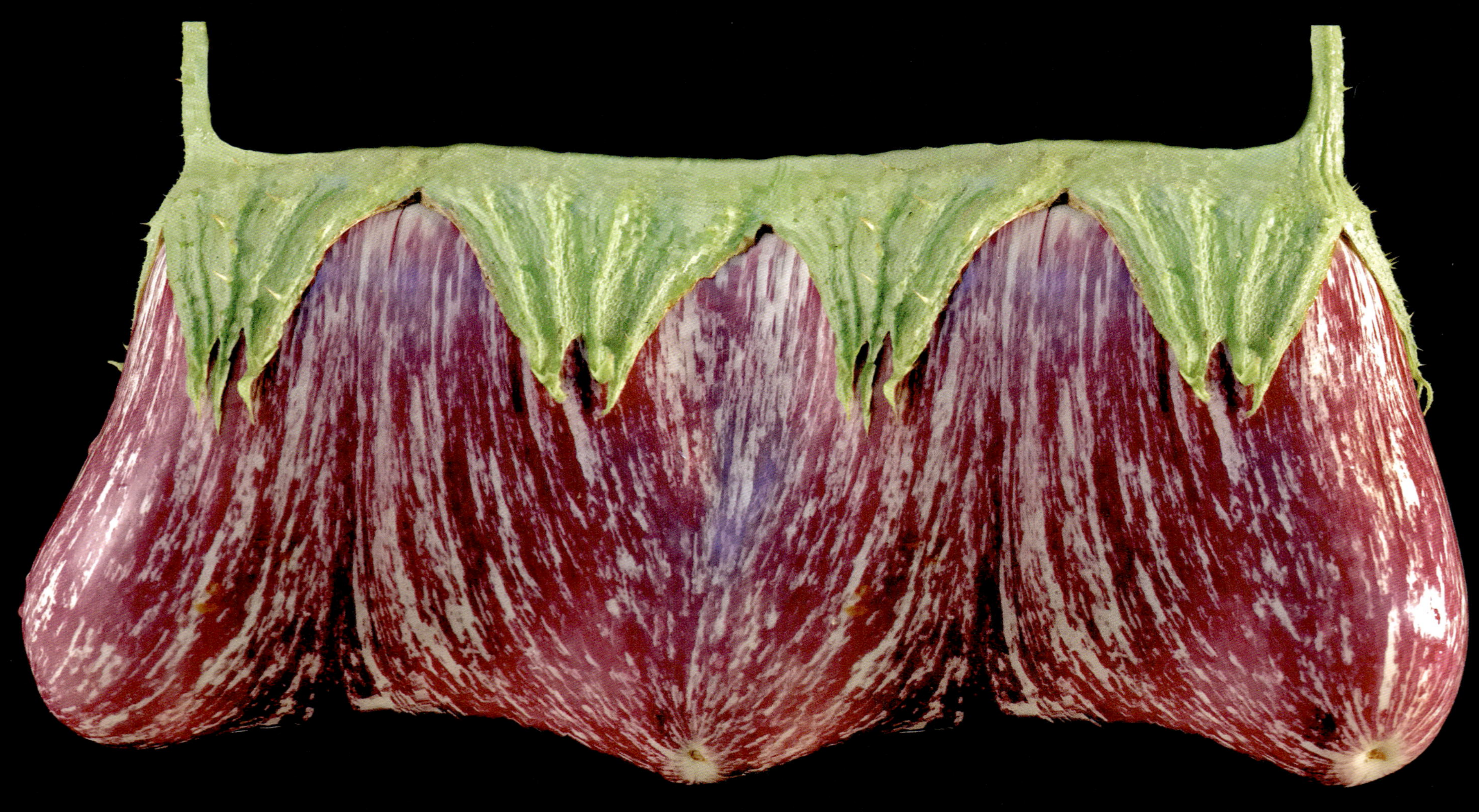

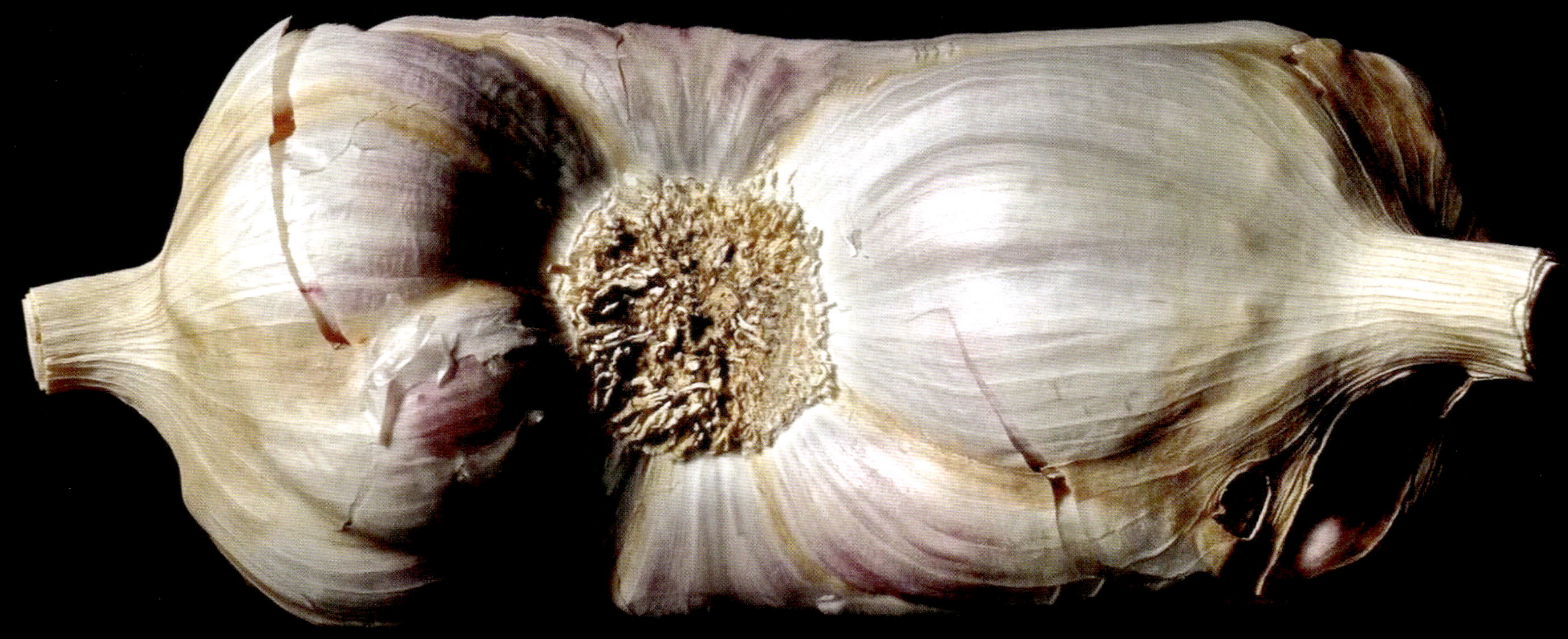

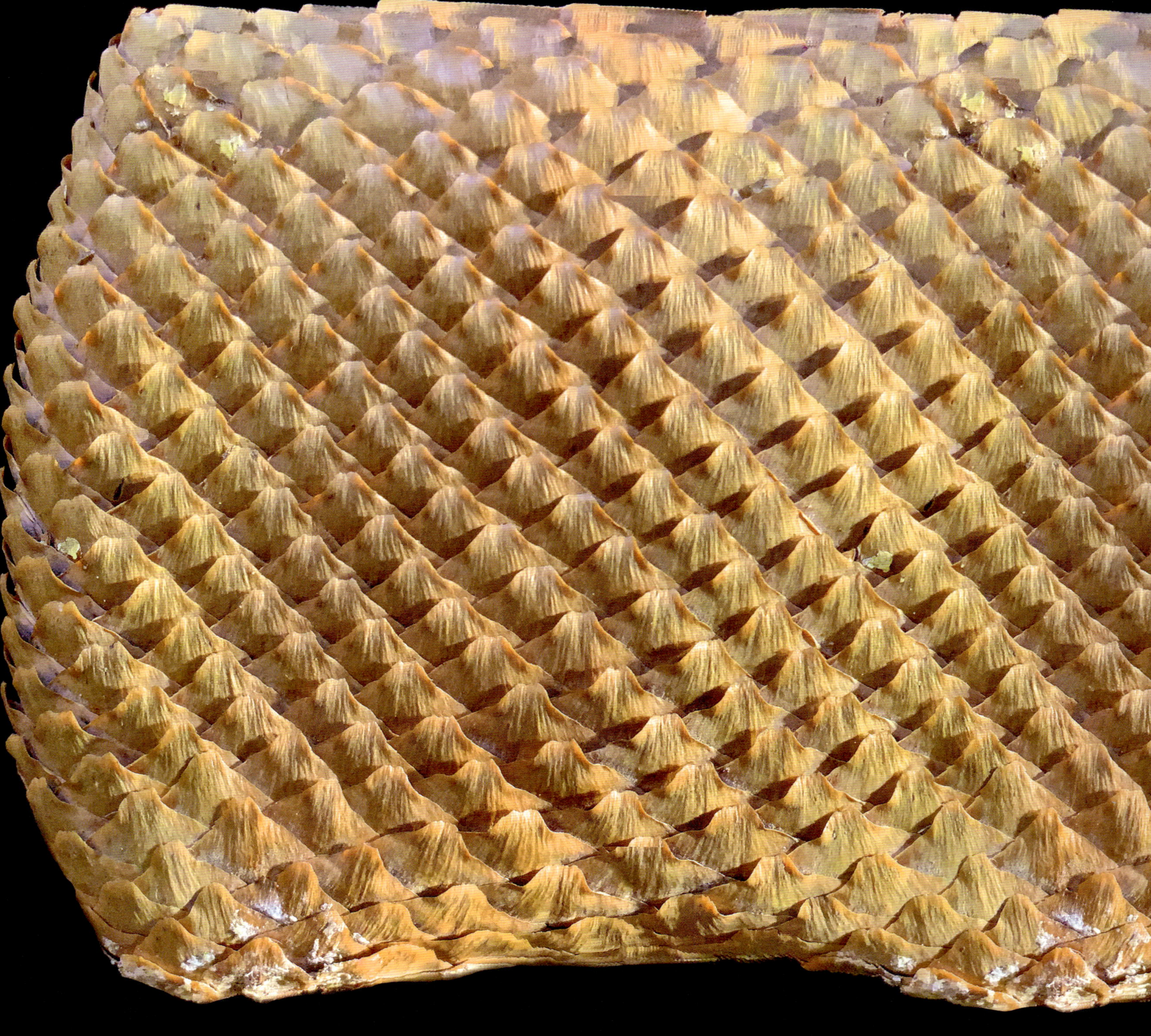

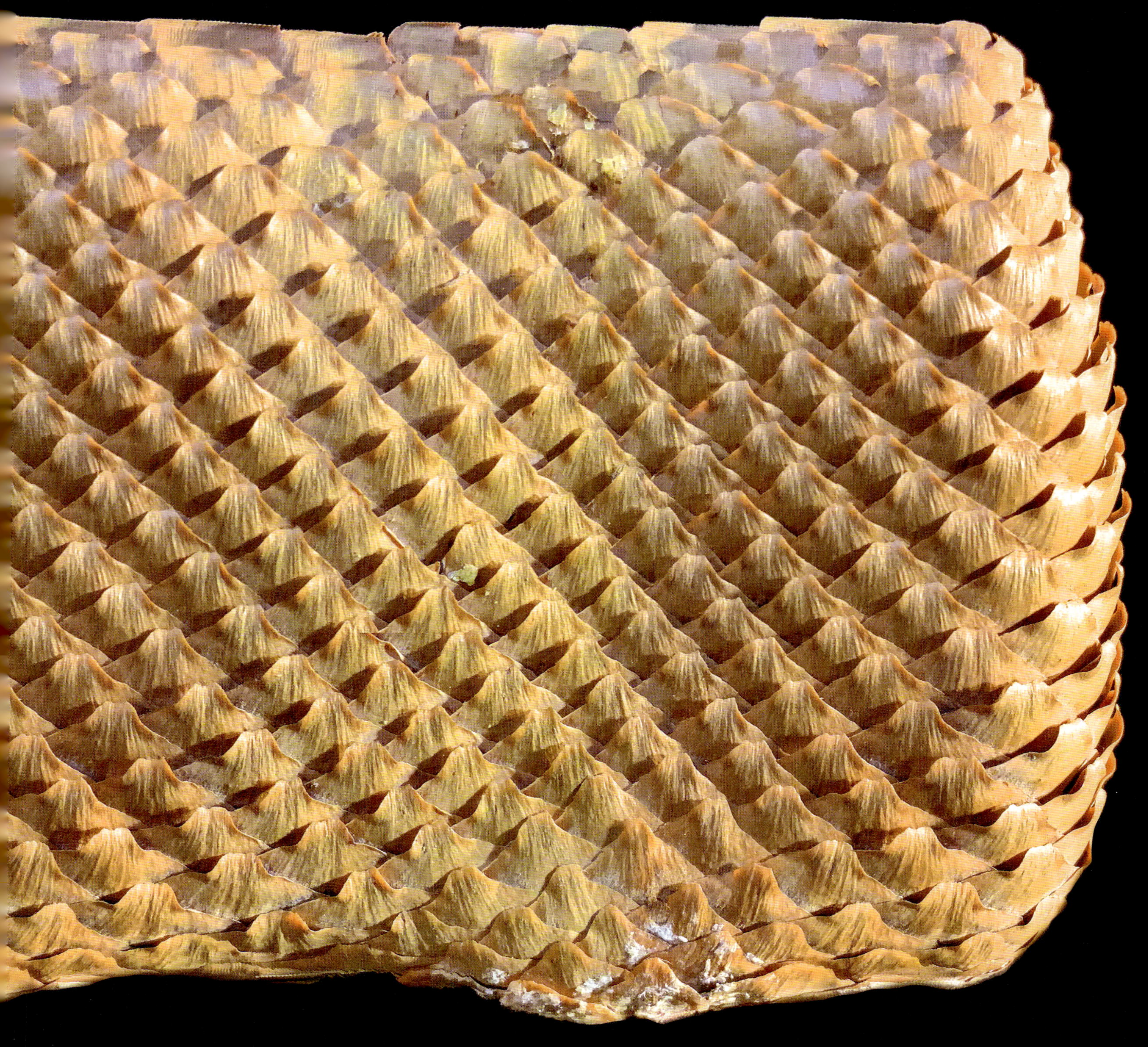

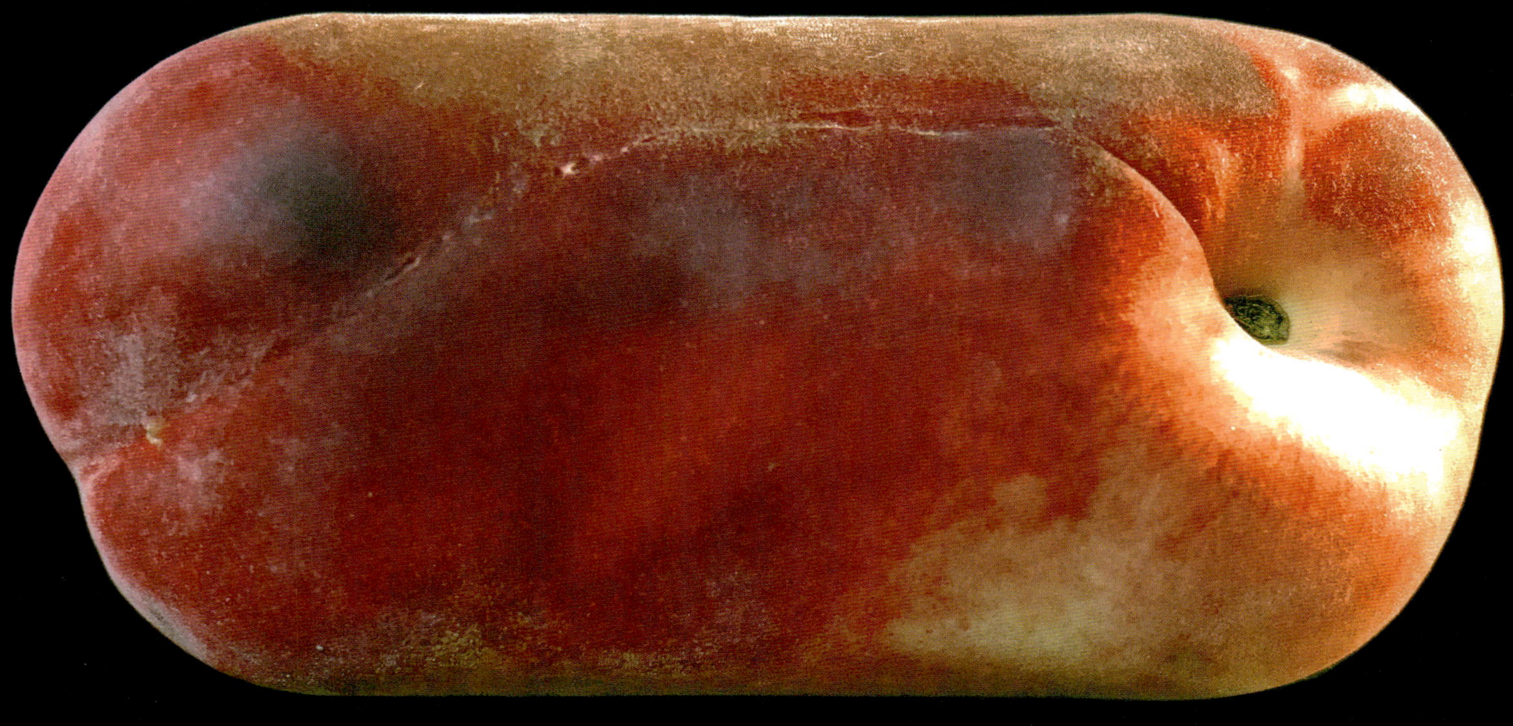

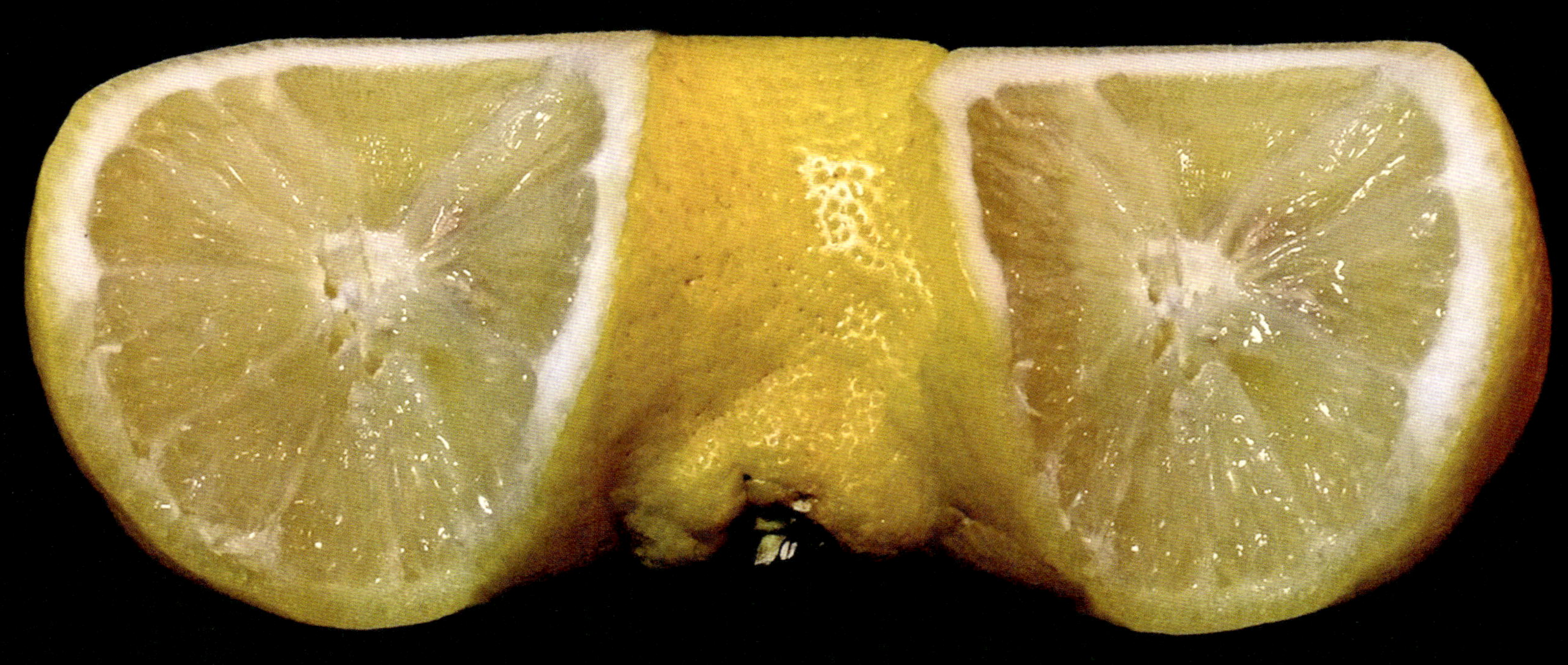

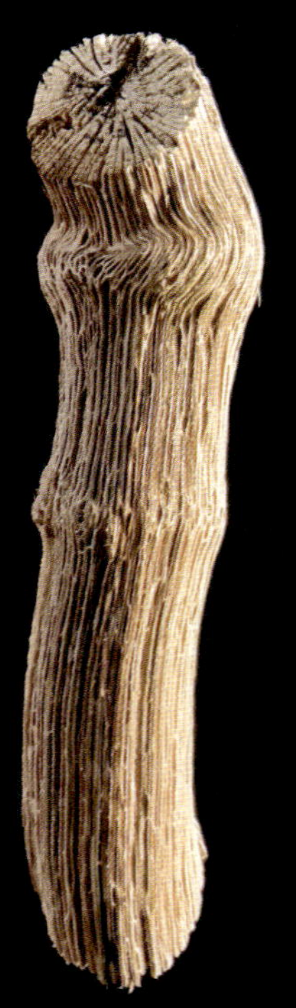
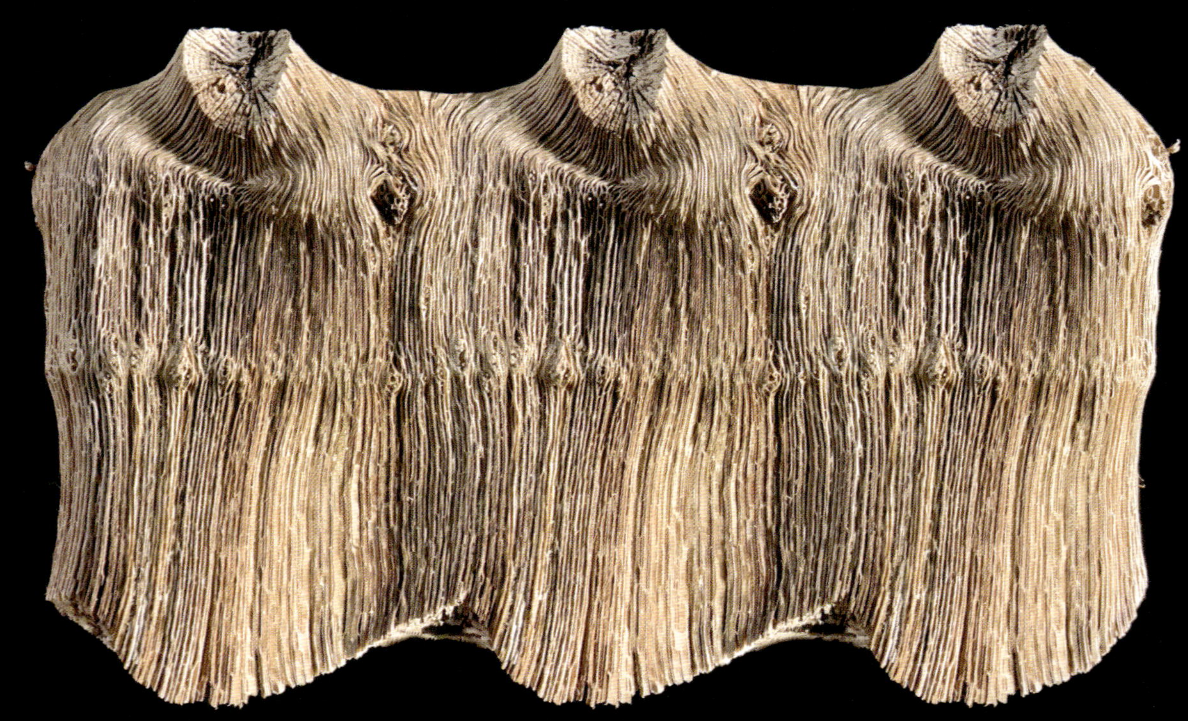

54

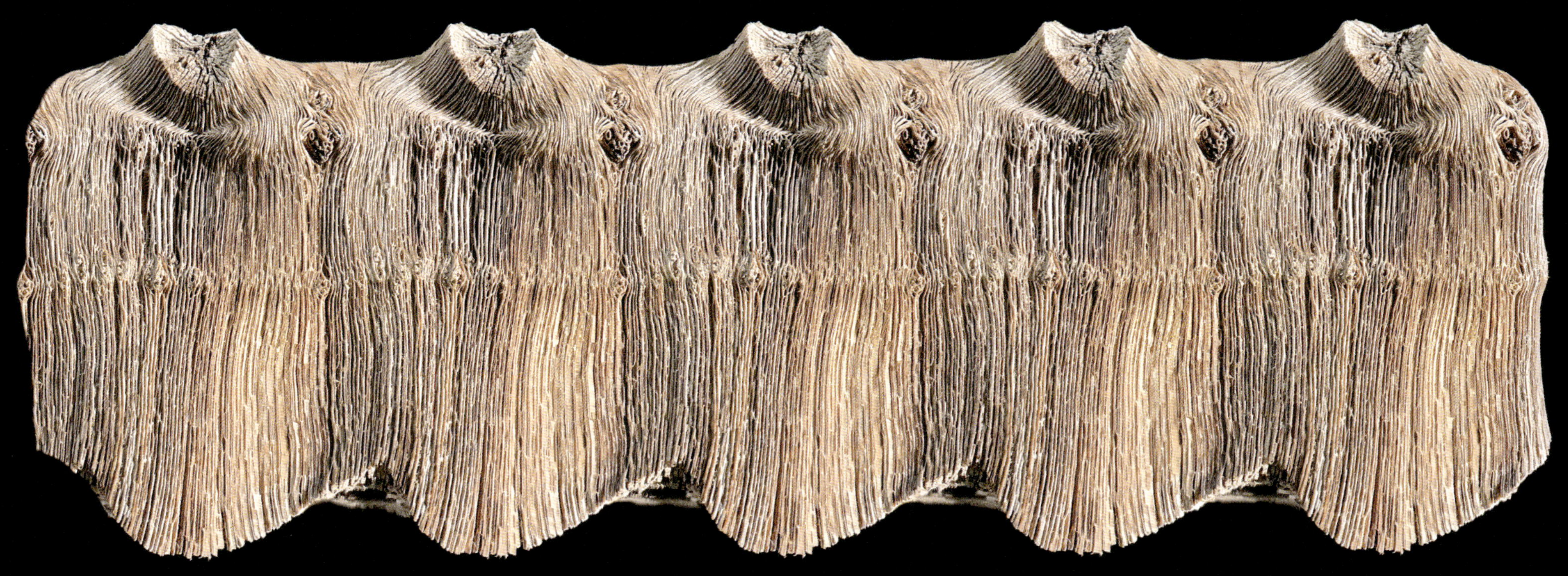

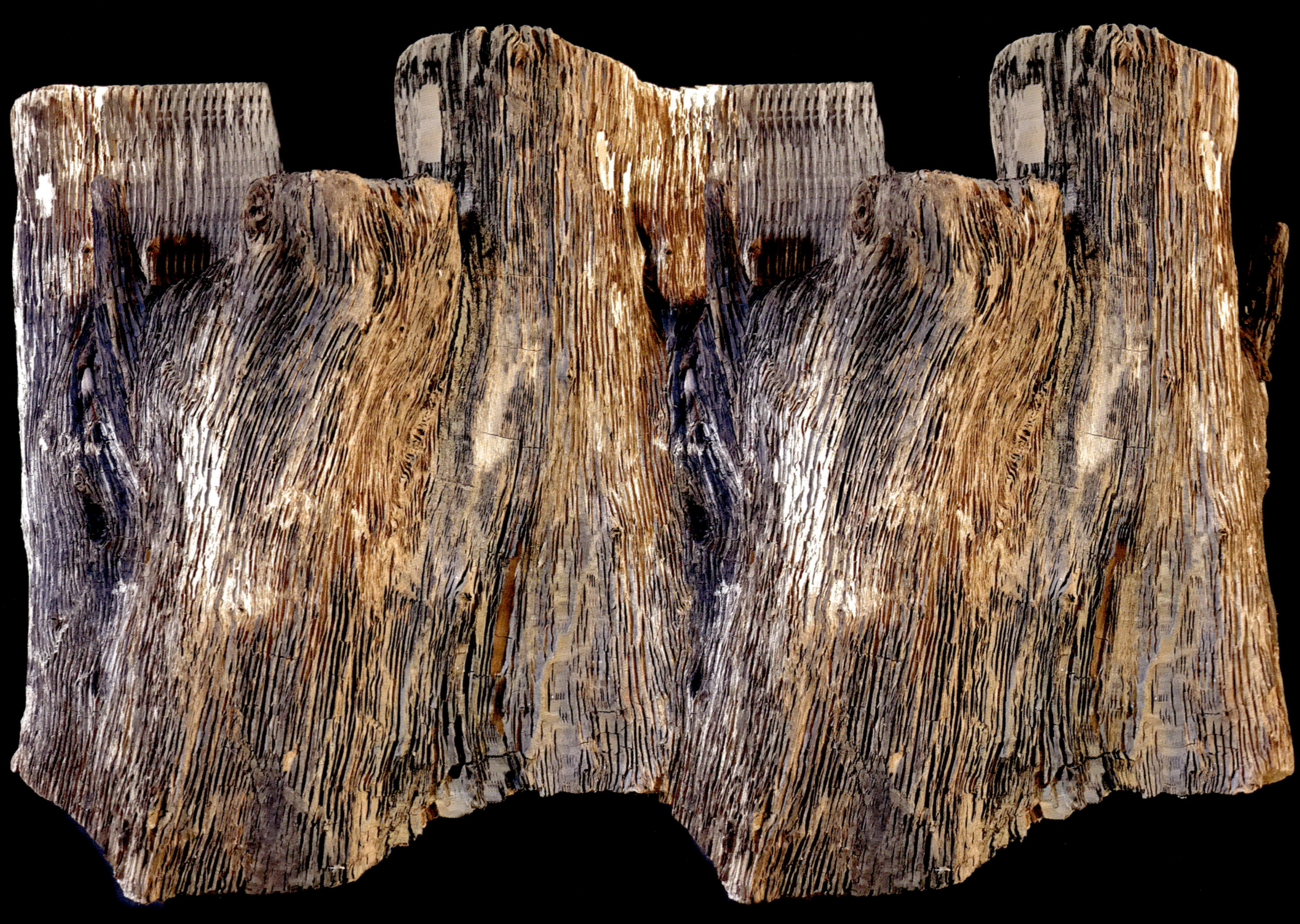

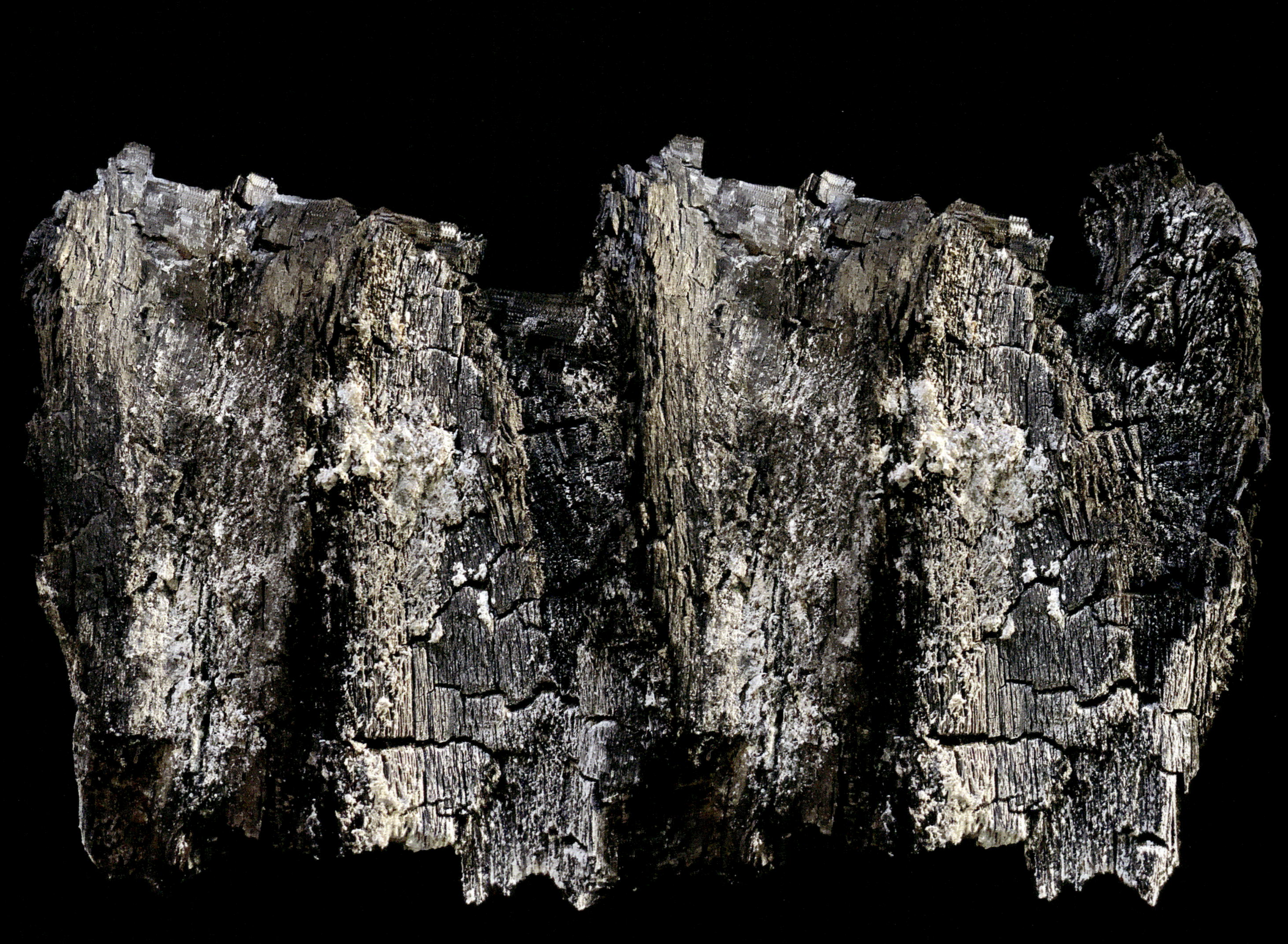

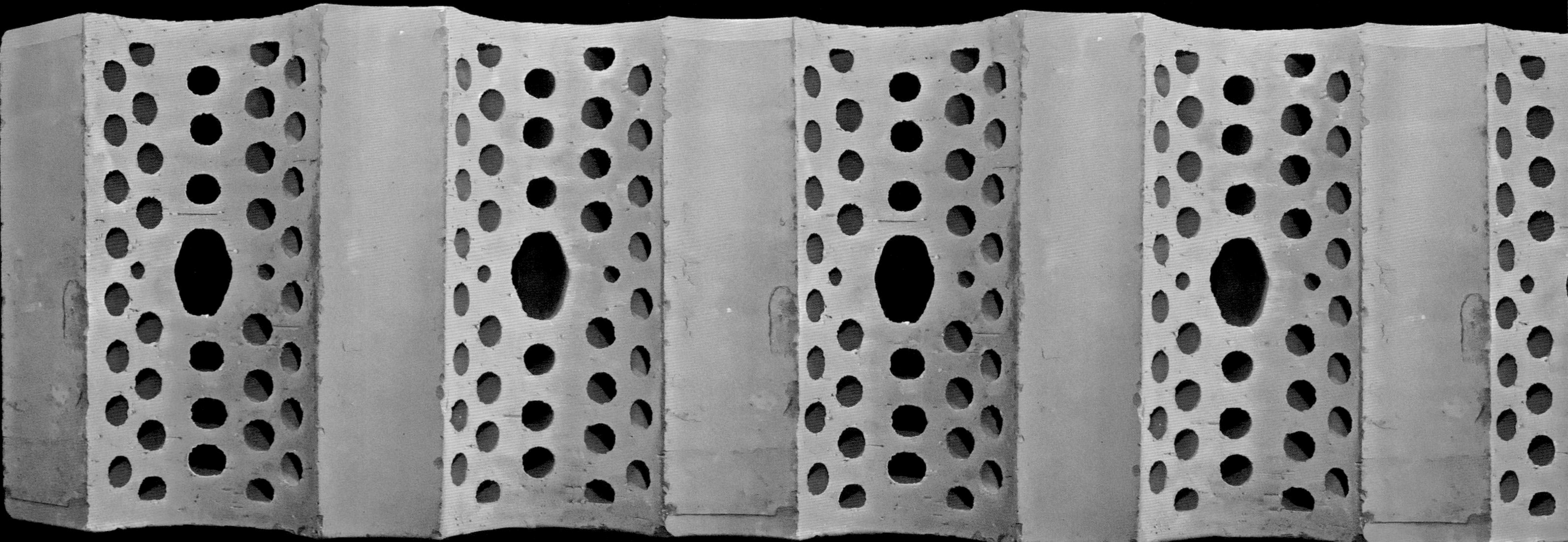

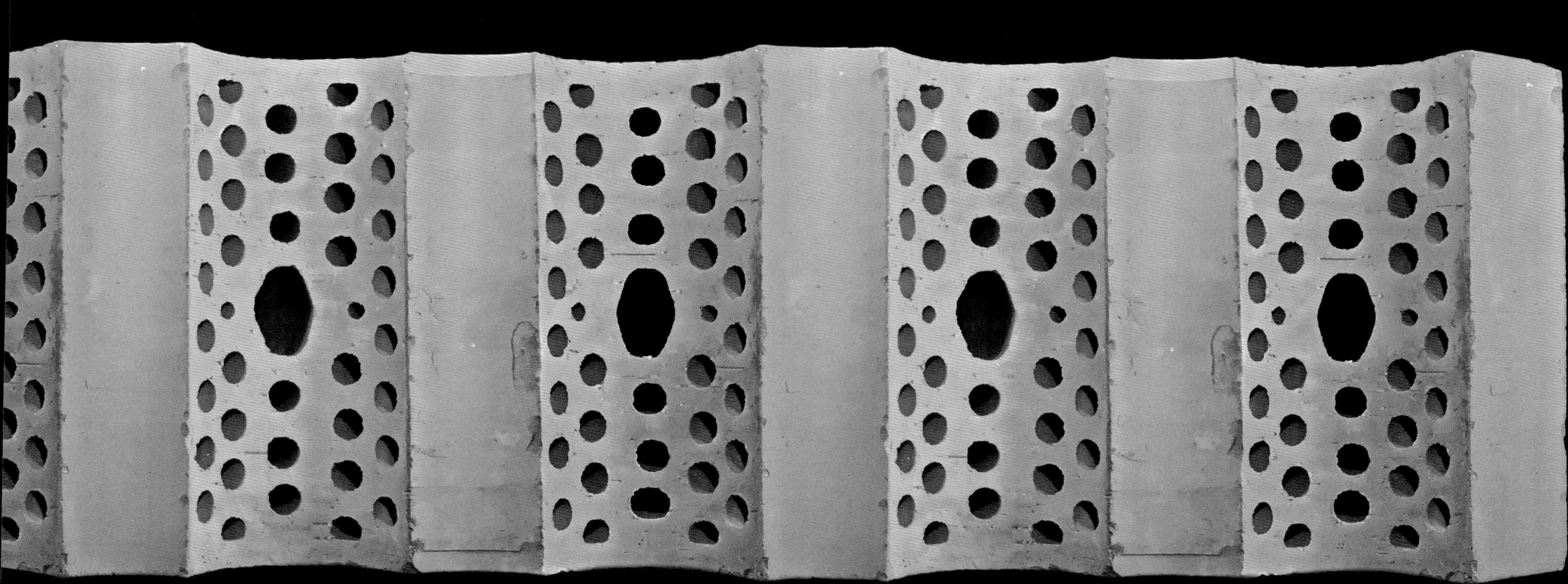

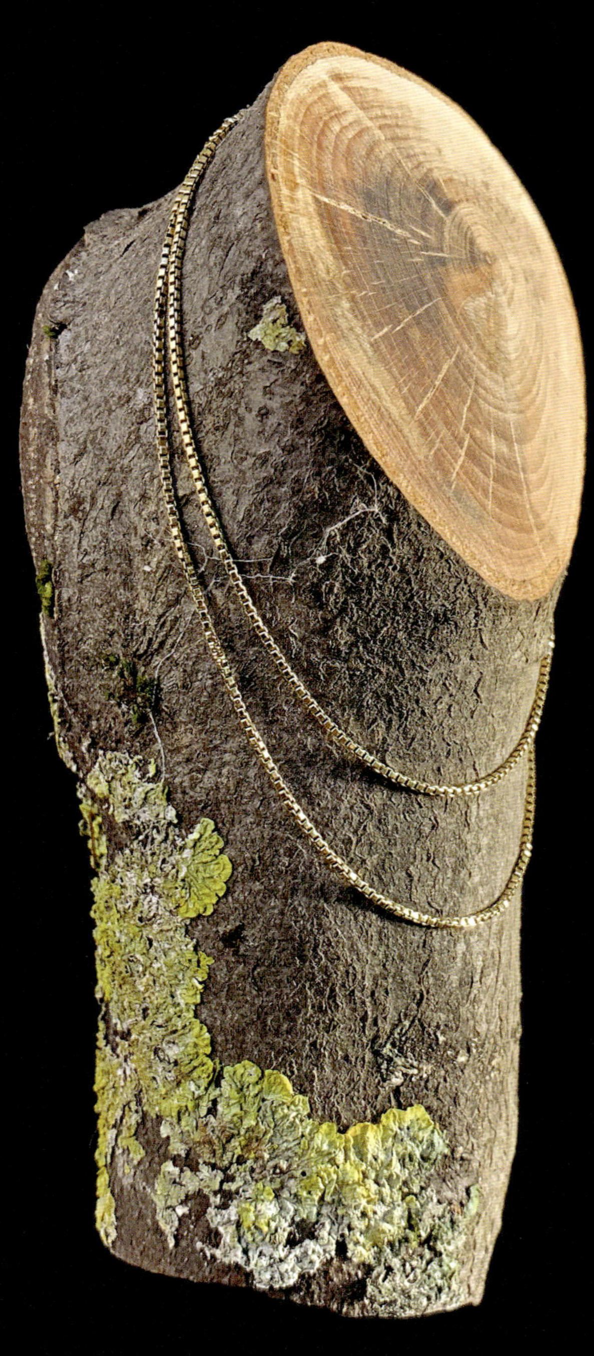

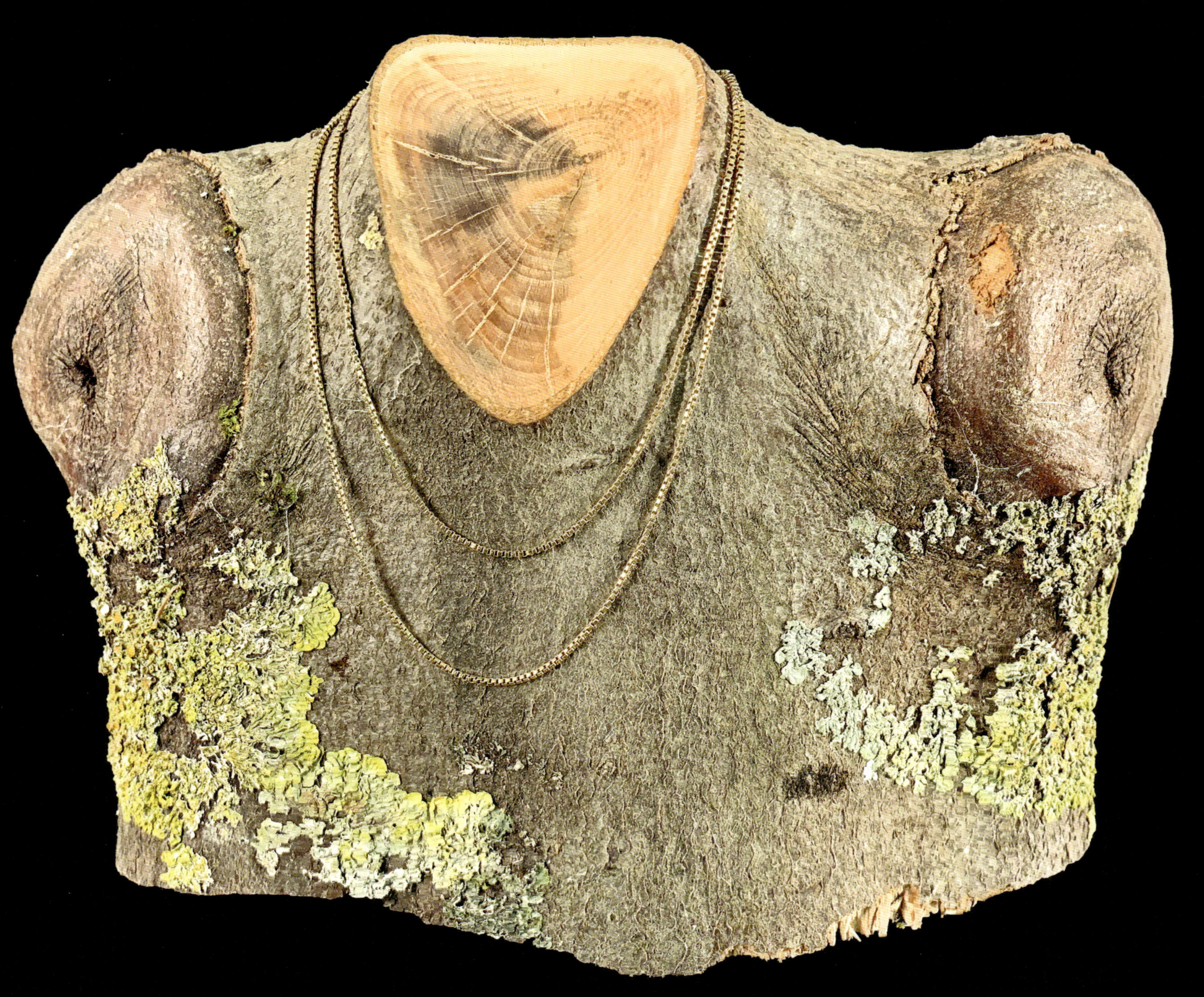

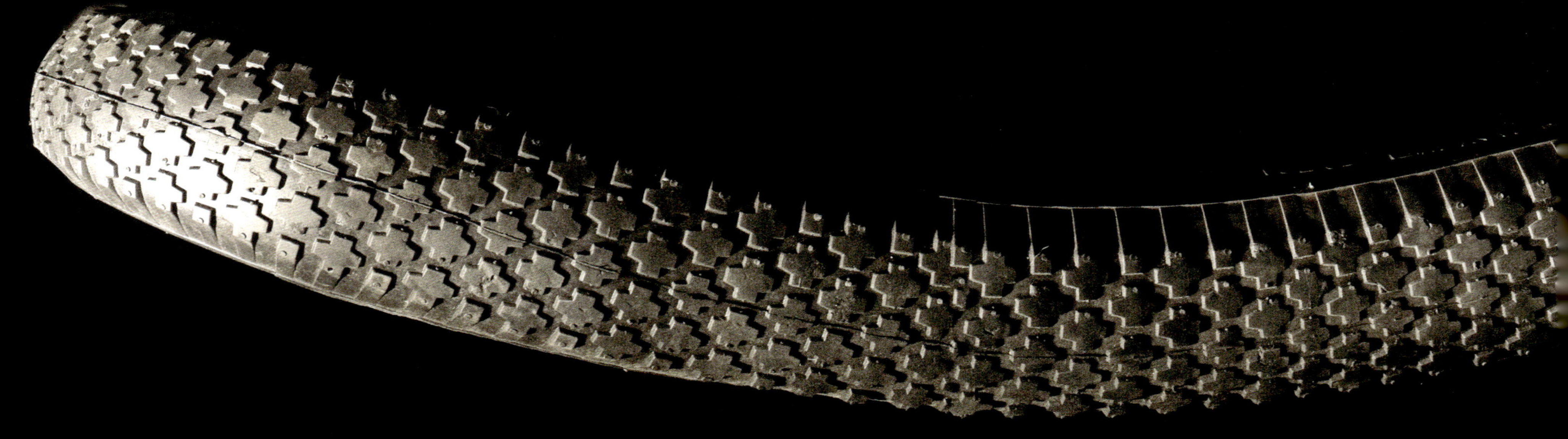

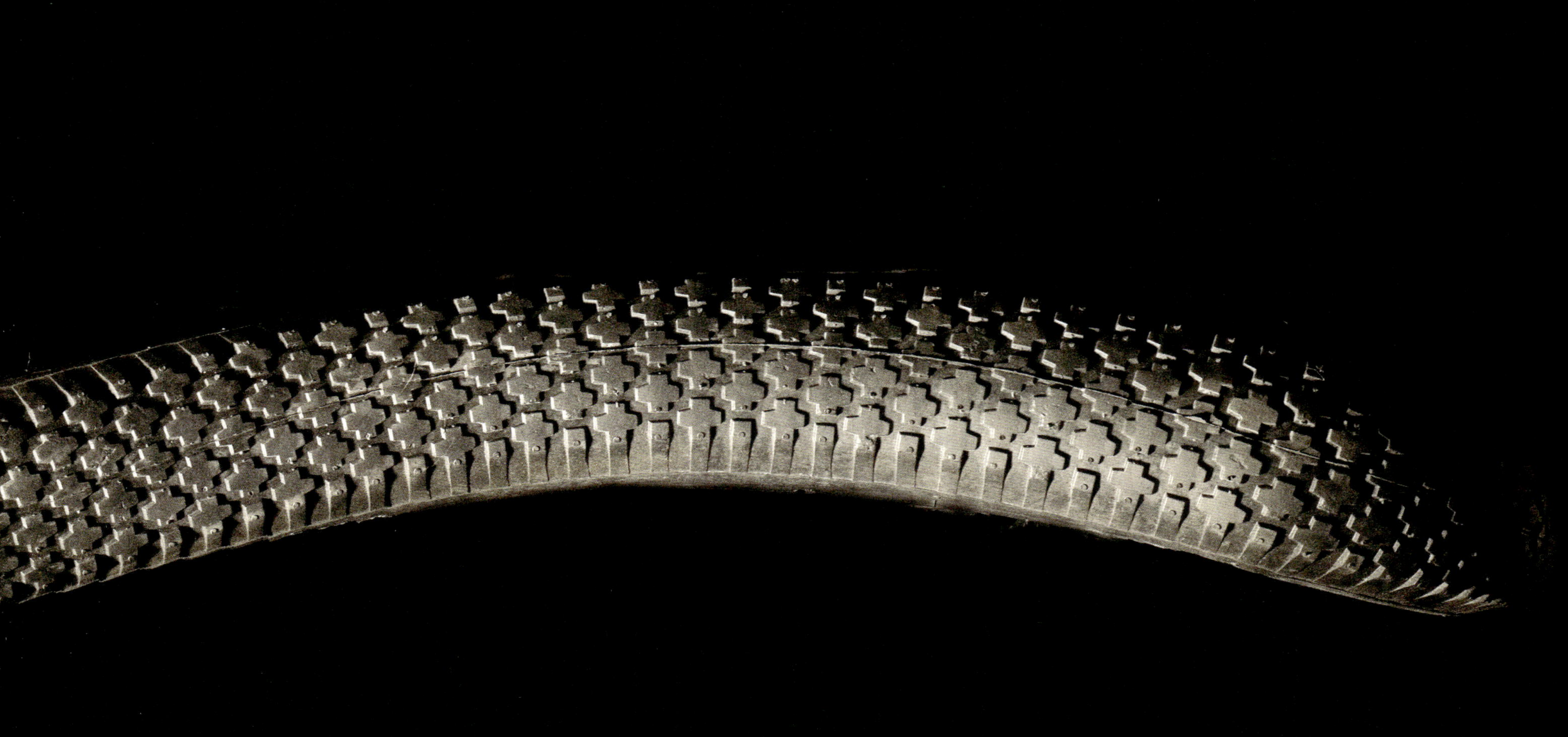

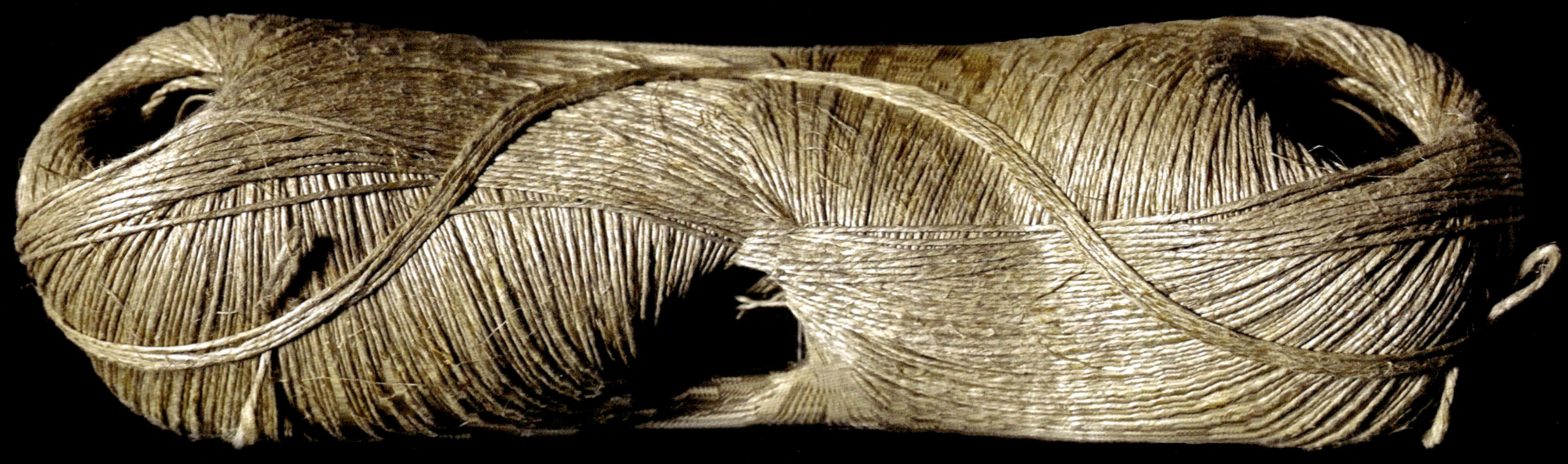

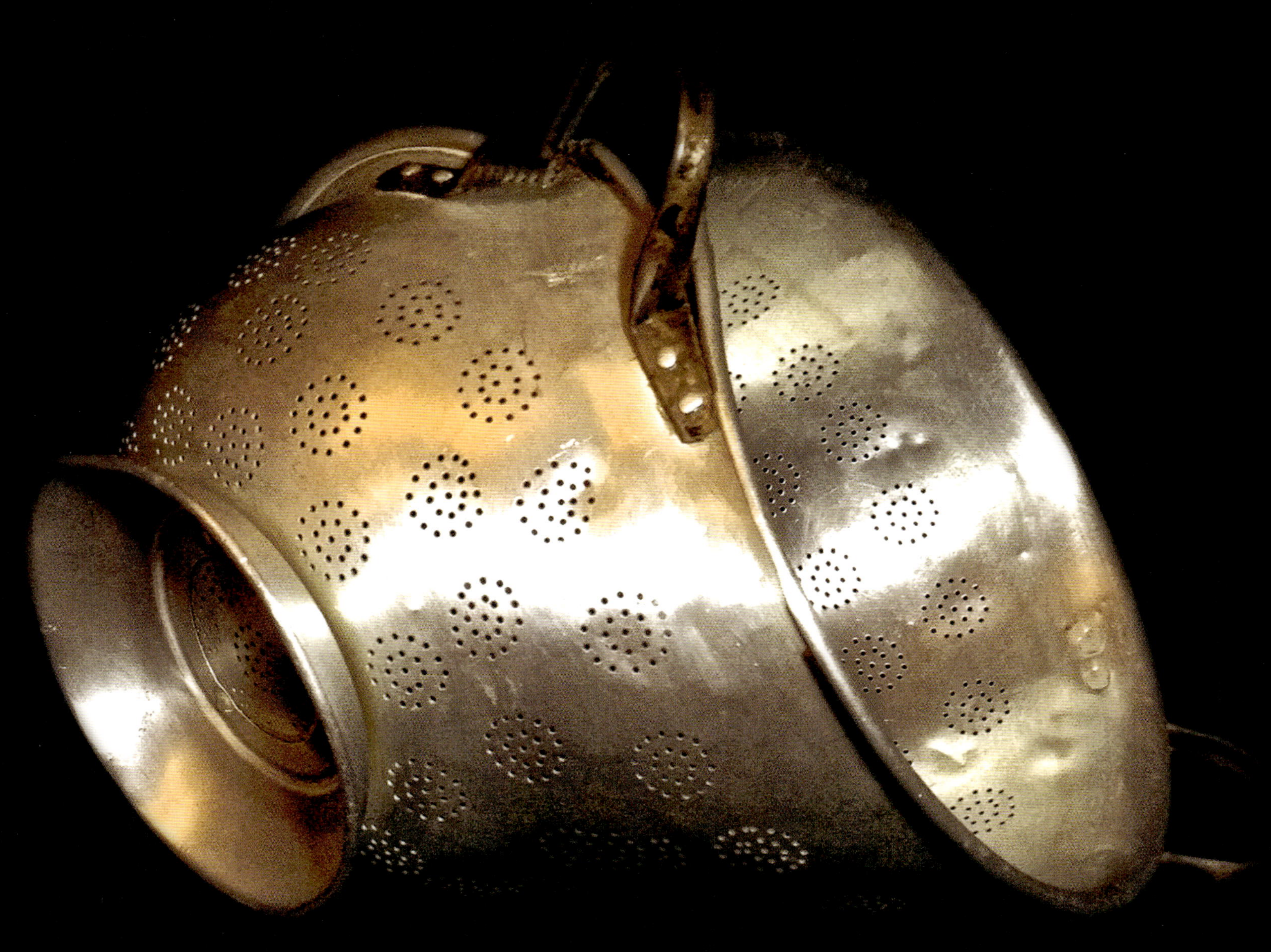

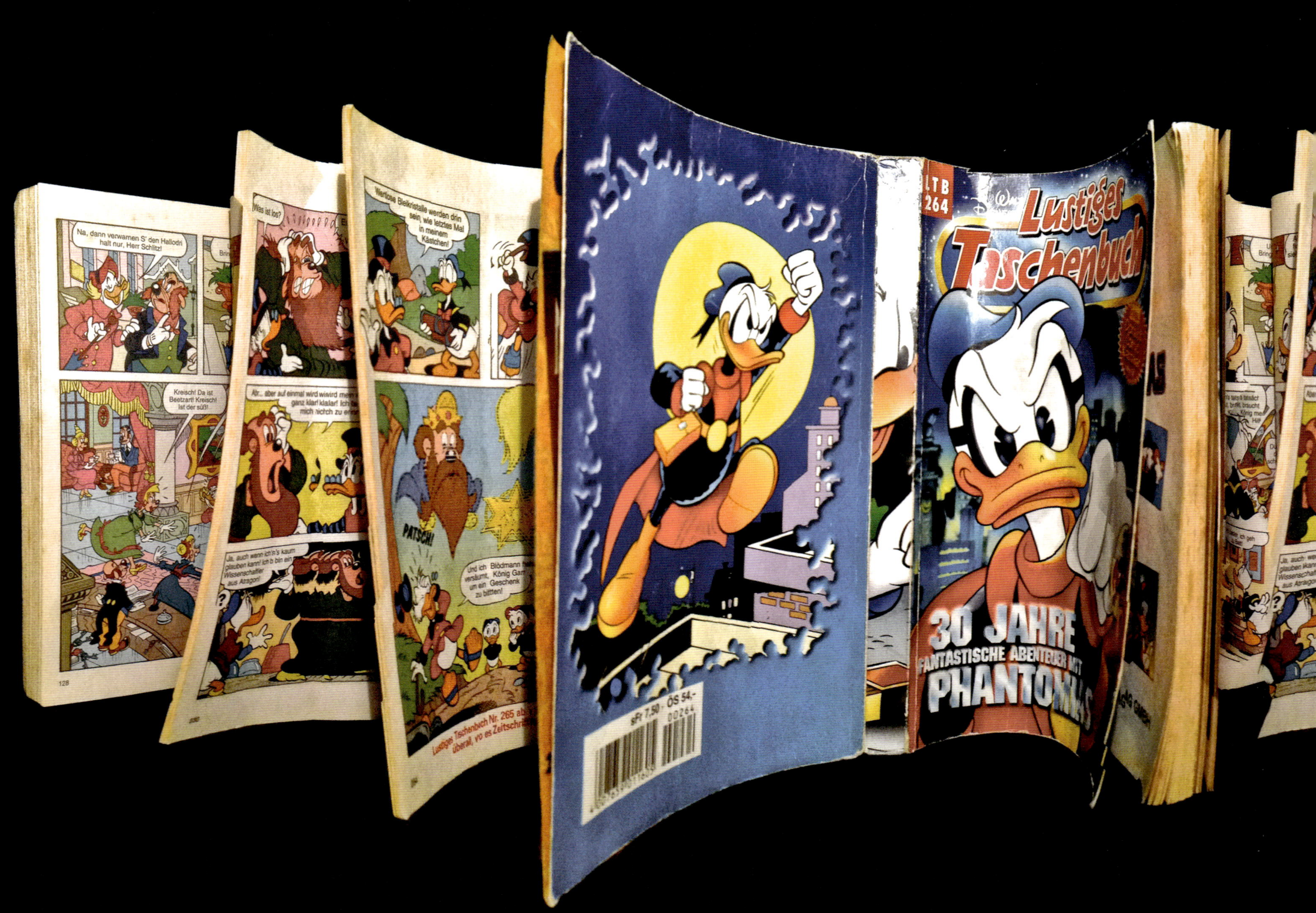
LTB 264
Walt Disney
Lustiges Taschenbuch
30 JAHRE
FANTASTISCHE ABENTEUER MIT
PHANTOMIAS
sFr. 7,50   ÖS 54,-

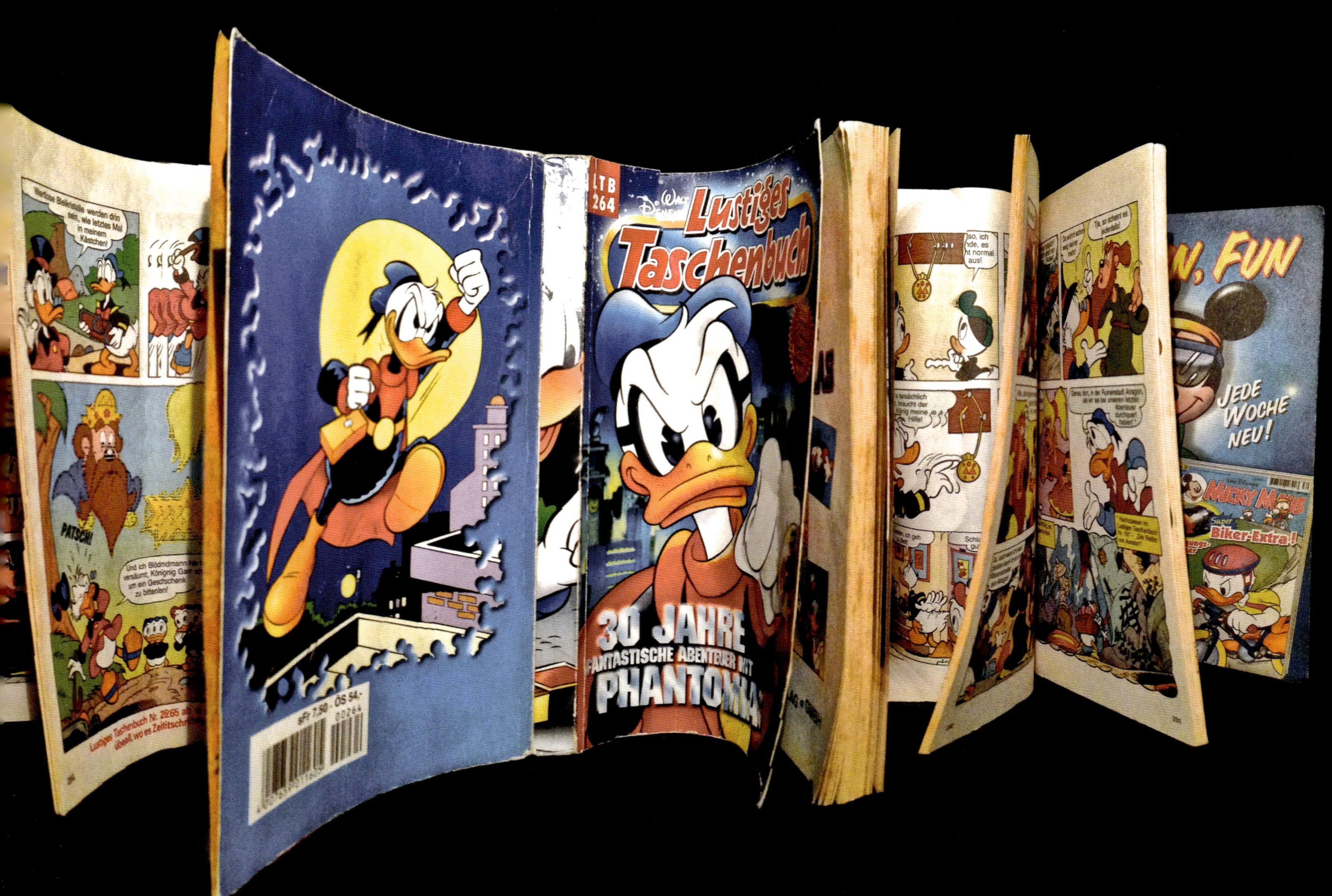
LTB
264
Lustiges Taschenbuch
30 JAHRE
FANTASTISCHE ABENTEUER MIT
PHANTOMIAS
sFr 7.50 - ÖS 54.-
00264
..N, FUN
JEDE
WOCHE
NEU!
MICKY MAUS
Super
Biker-Extra!

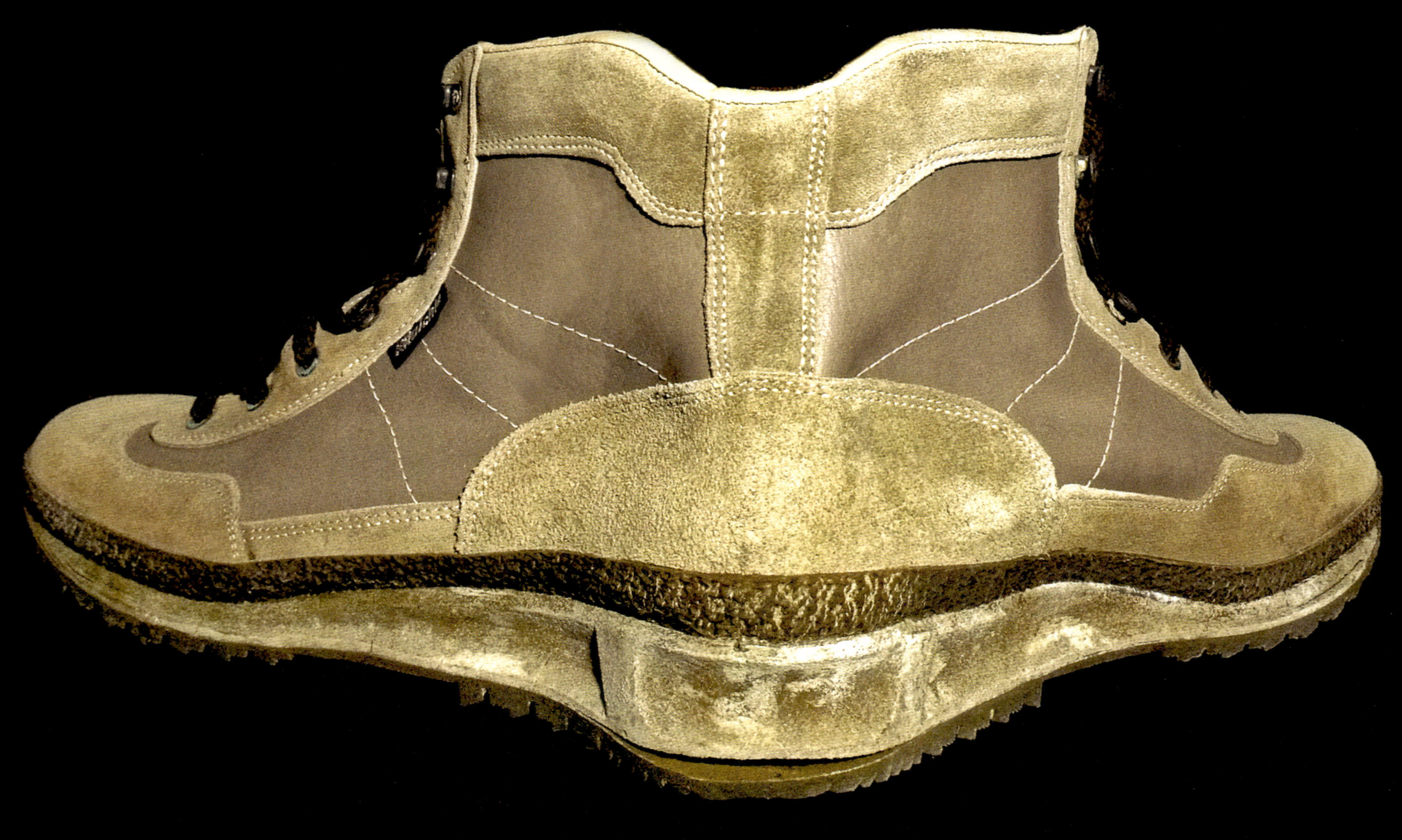

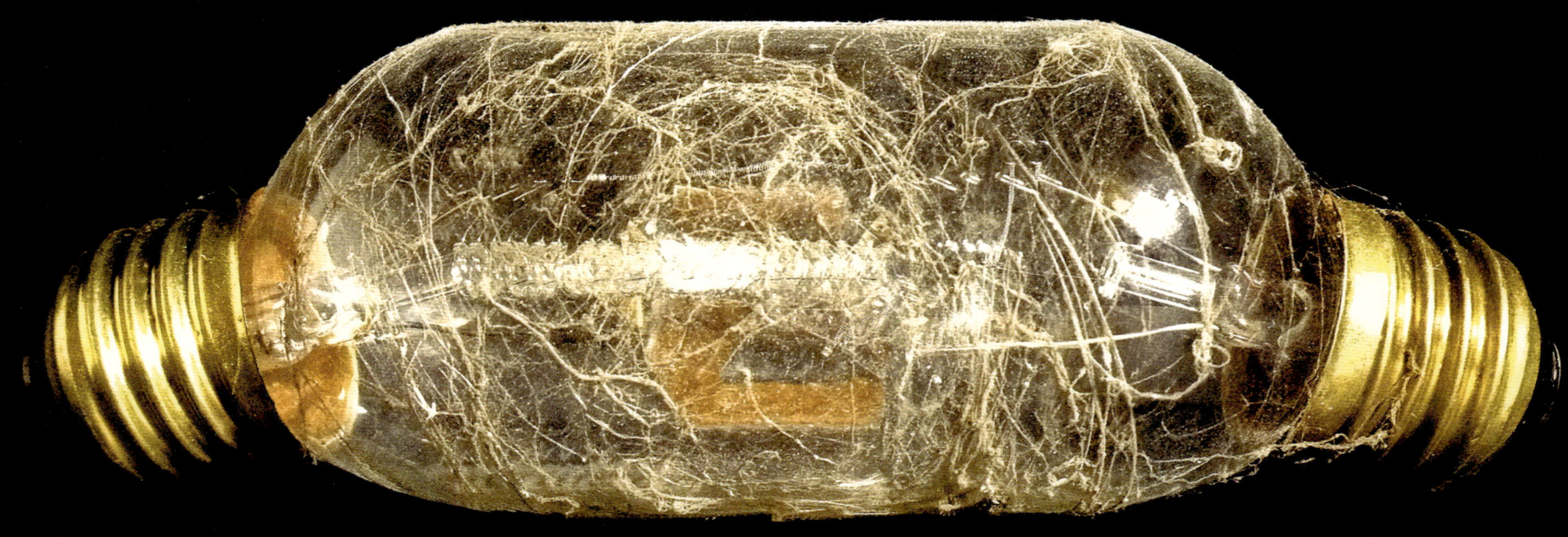

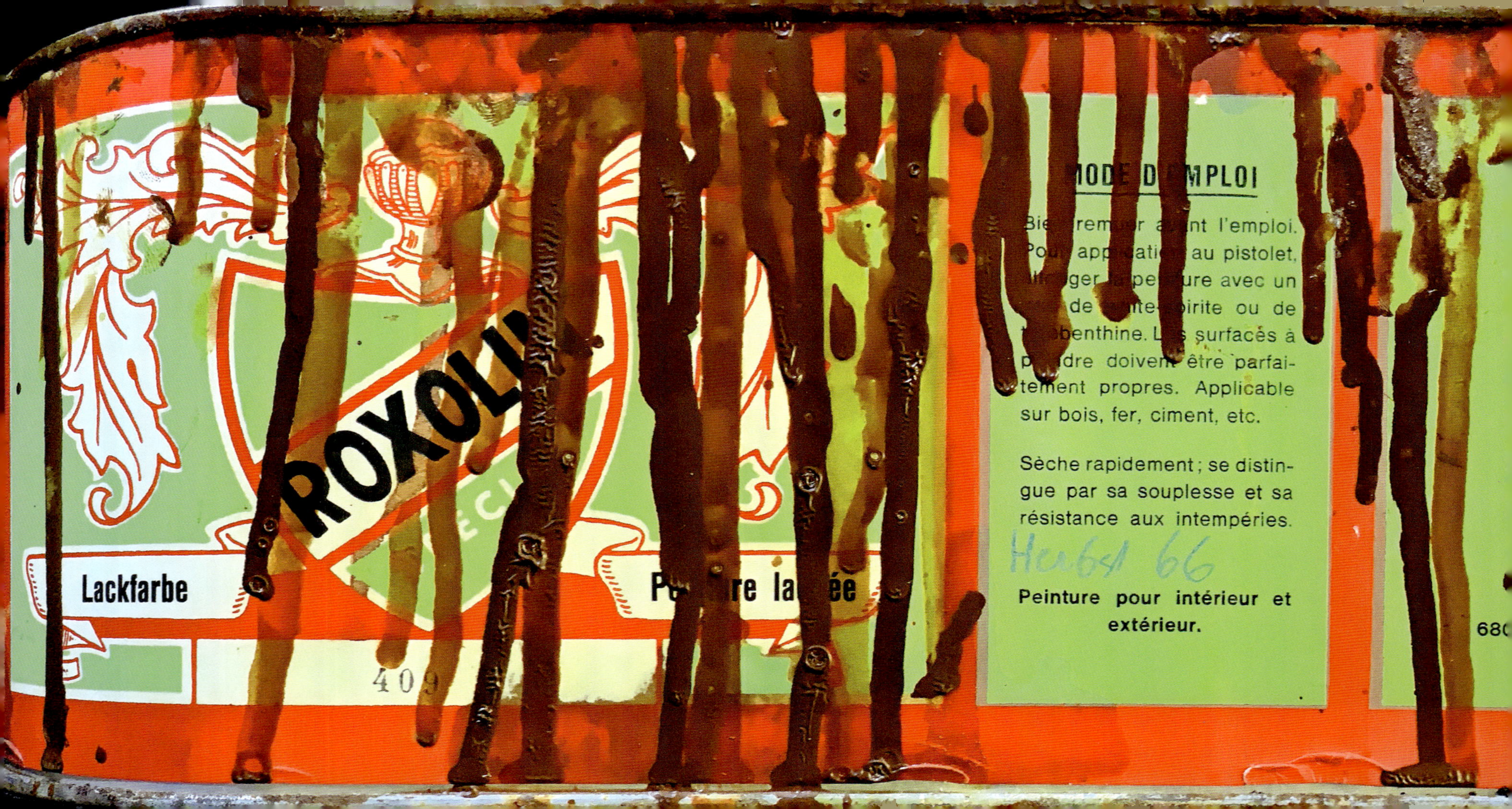
ROXOLI
Lackfarbe
Peinture laquée
MODE D'EMPLOI
Bien remuer avant l'emploi.
Pour application au pistolet,
allonger la peinture avec un
de white-spirit ou de
térébenthine. Les surfaces à
peindre doivent être parfai-
tement propres. Applicable
sur bois, fer, ciment, etc.

Sèche rapidement; se distin-
gue par sa souplesse et sa
résistance aux intempéries.
Herbst 66
Peinture pour intérieur et
extérieur.
409
680

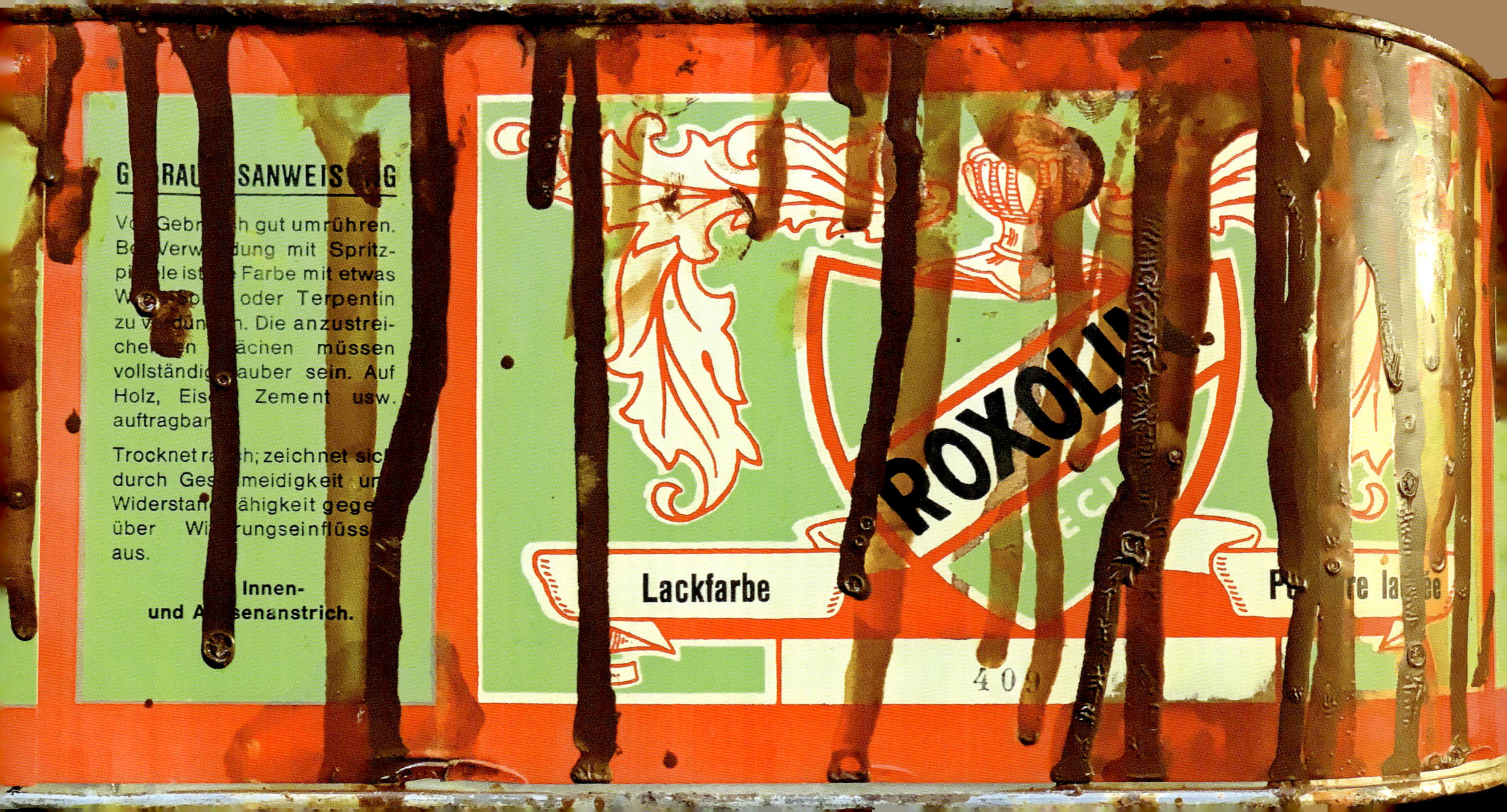
GEBRAUCHSANWEISUNG
Vor Gebrauch gut umrühren.
Bei Verwendung mit Spritz-
pistole ist die Farbe mit etwas
Weissspr. oder Terpentin
zu verdünnen. Die anzustrei-
chenden Flächen müssen
vollständig sauber sein. Auf
Holz, Eisen, Zement usw.
auftragbar.
Trocknet rasch; zeichnet sich
durch Geschmeidigkeit und
Widerstandsfähigkeit gegen-
über Witterungseinflüssen
aus.
Innen-
und Aussenanstrich.
ROXOLIN
Lackfarbe
Peinture laquée
409

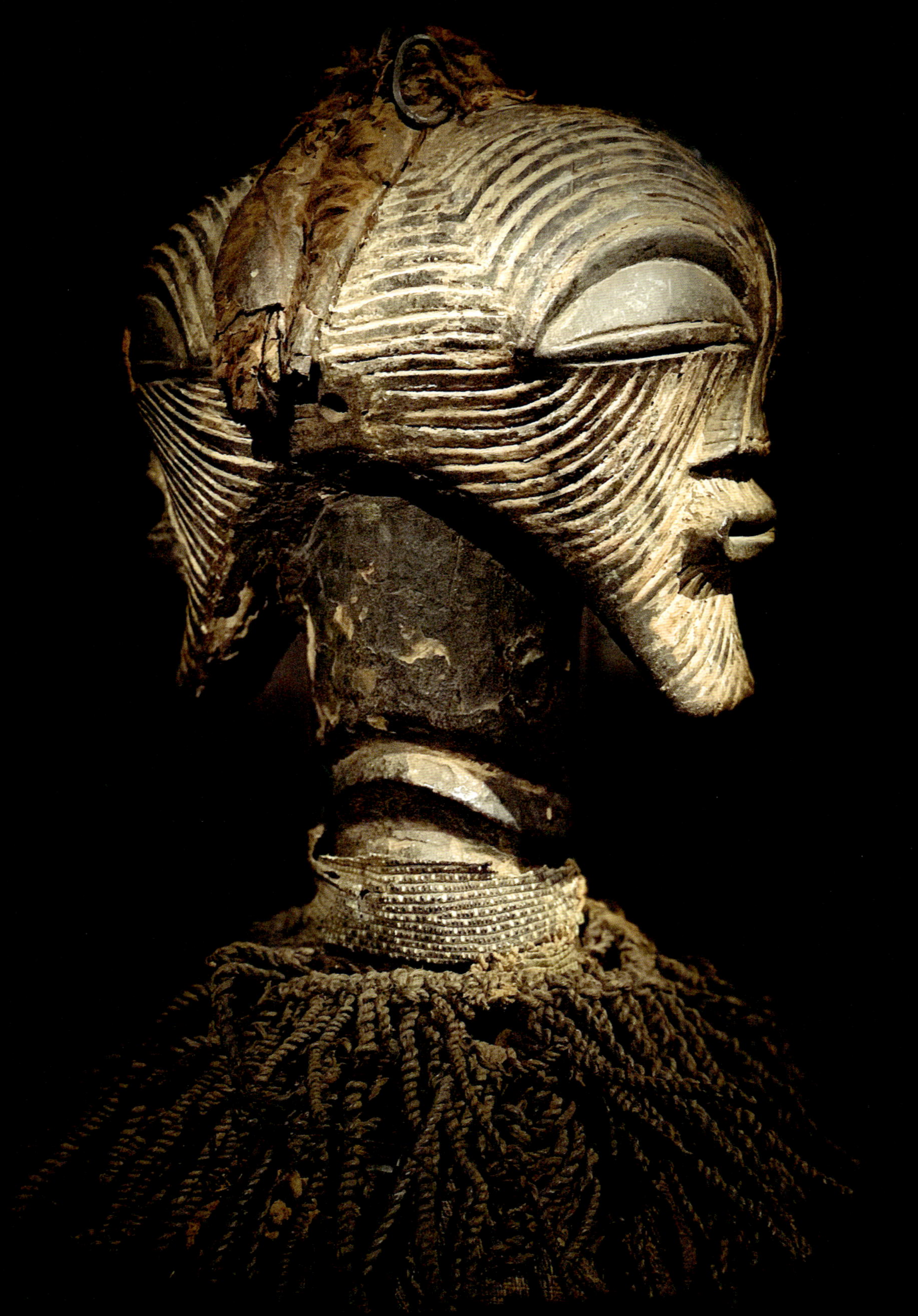

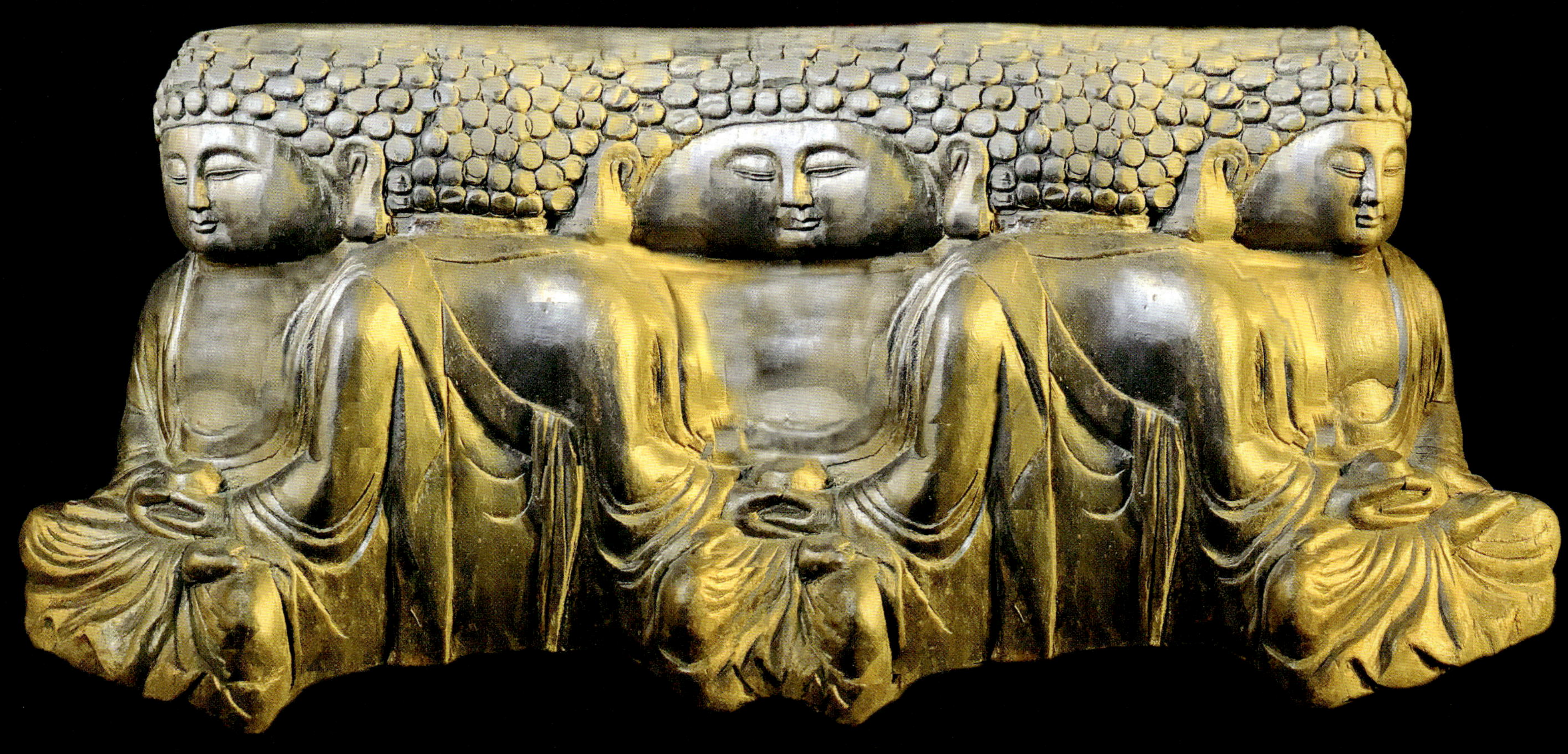

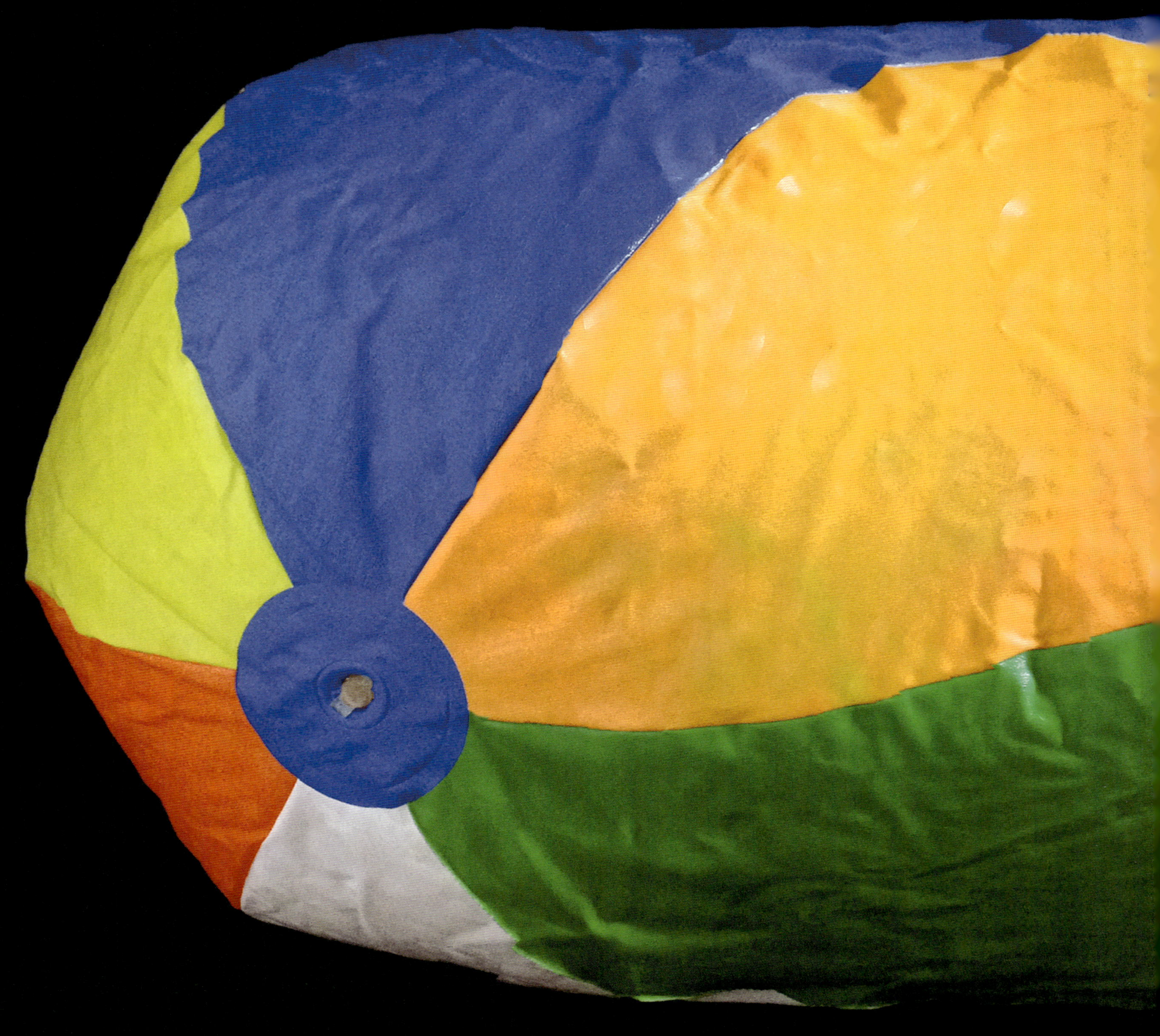

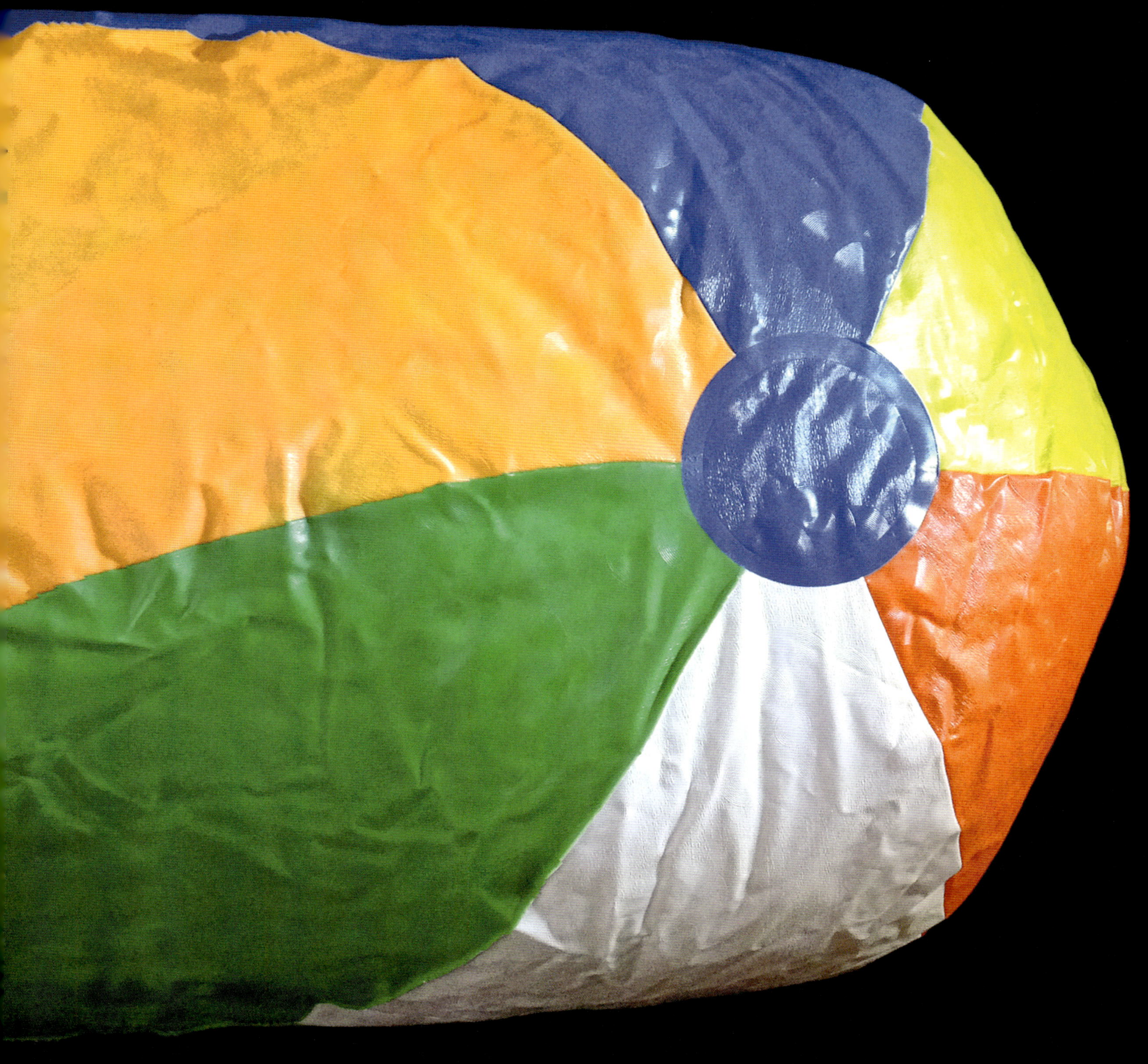

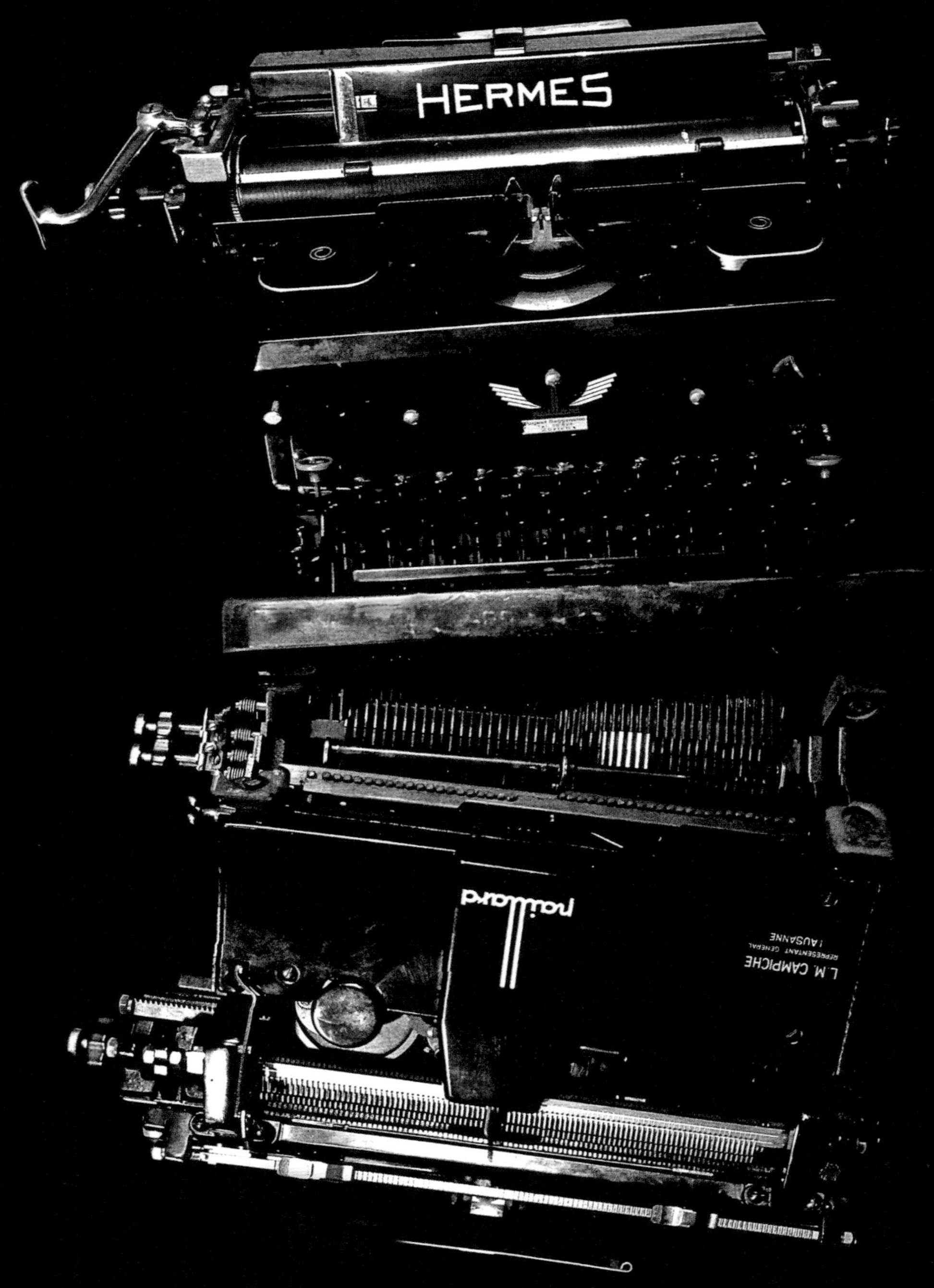

HERMES
Paillard
L.M CAMPICHE
REPRÉSENTANT GÉNÉRAL
LAUSANNE

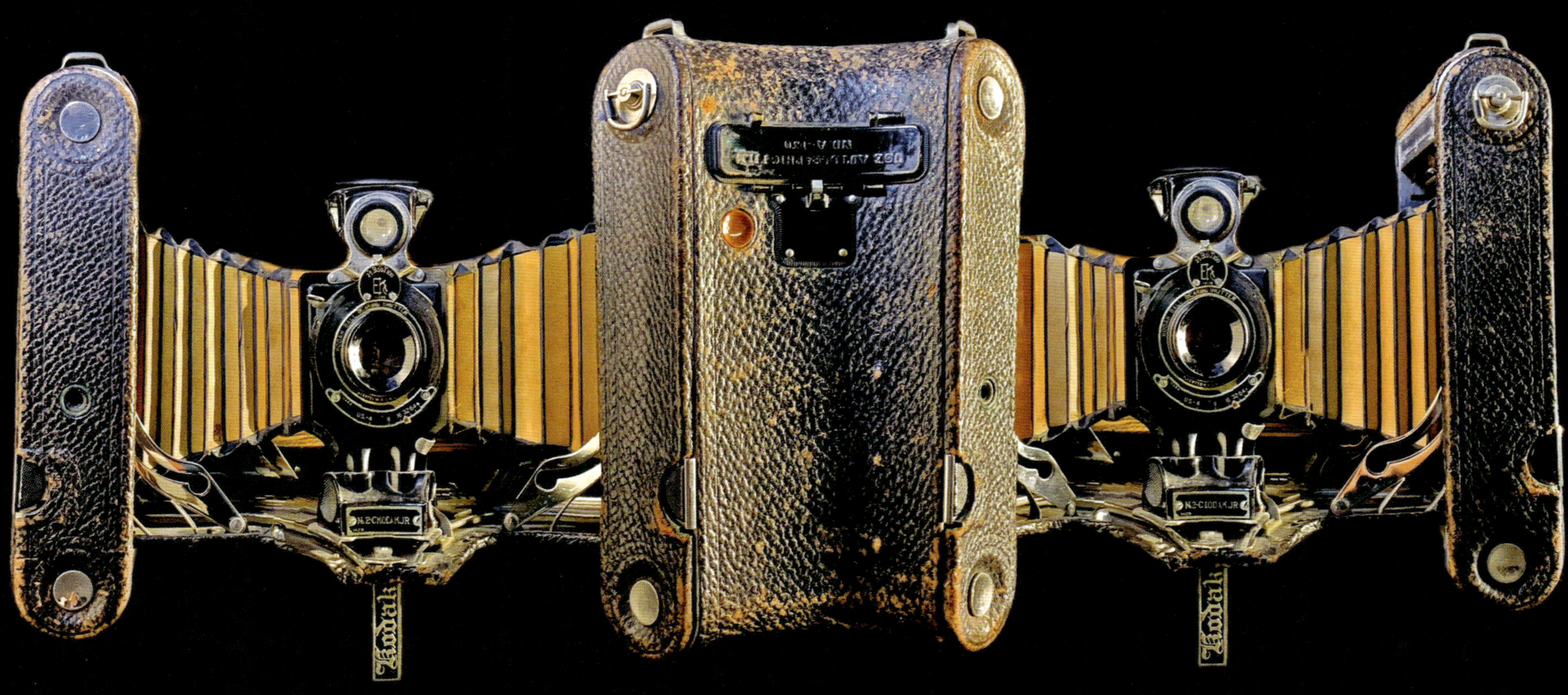

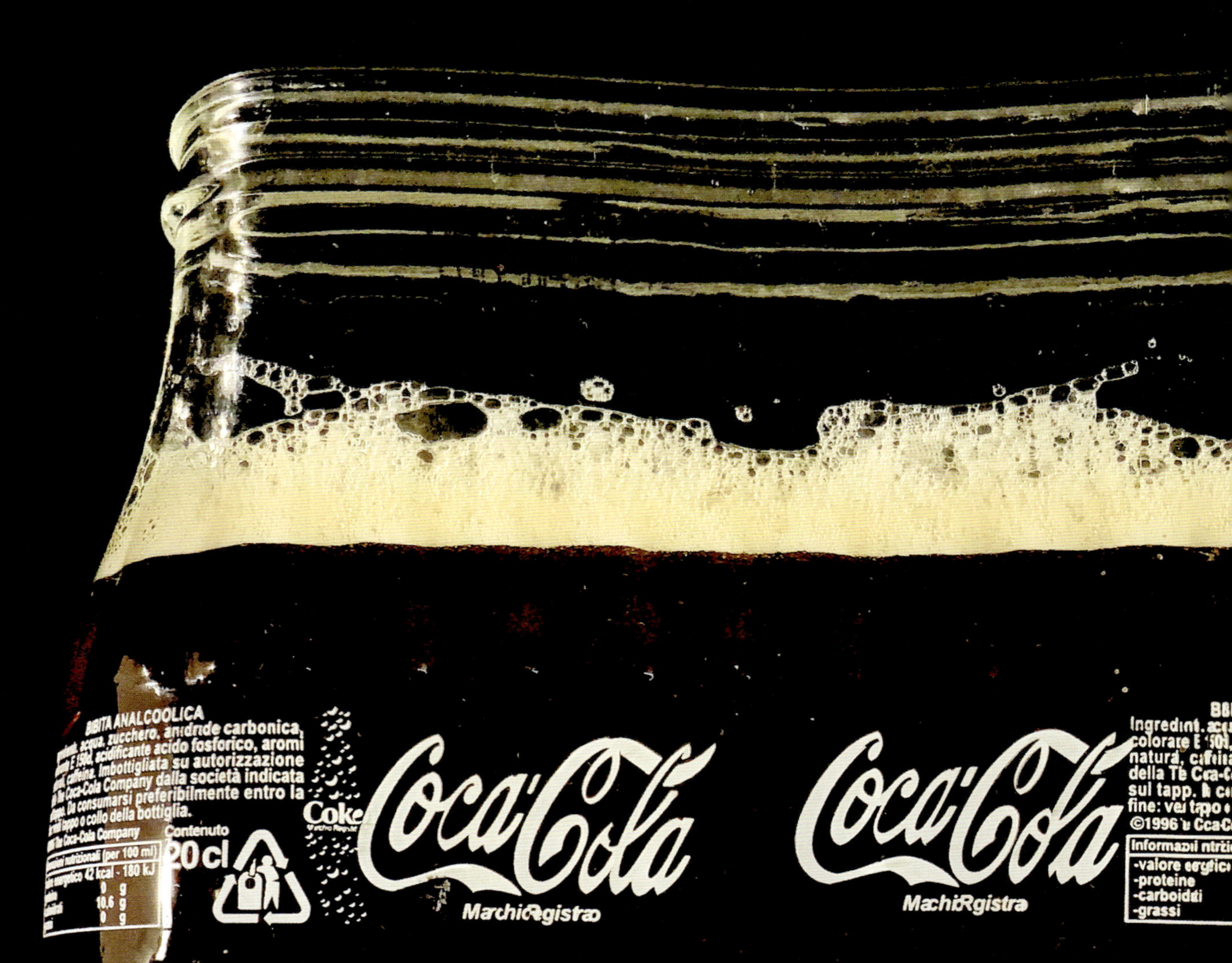

BIBITA ANALCOOLICA
Coca-Cola
Marchio Registrato
Coca-Cola
Marchio Registrato
Coke
20 cl
Contenuto
©1996 The Coca-Cola Company

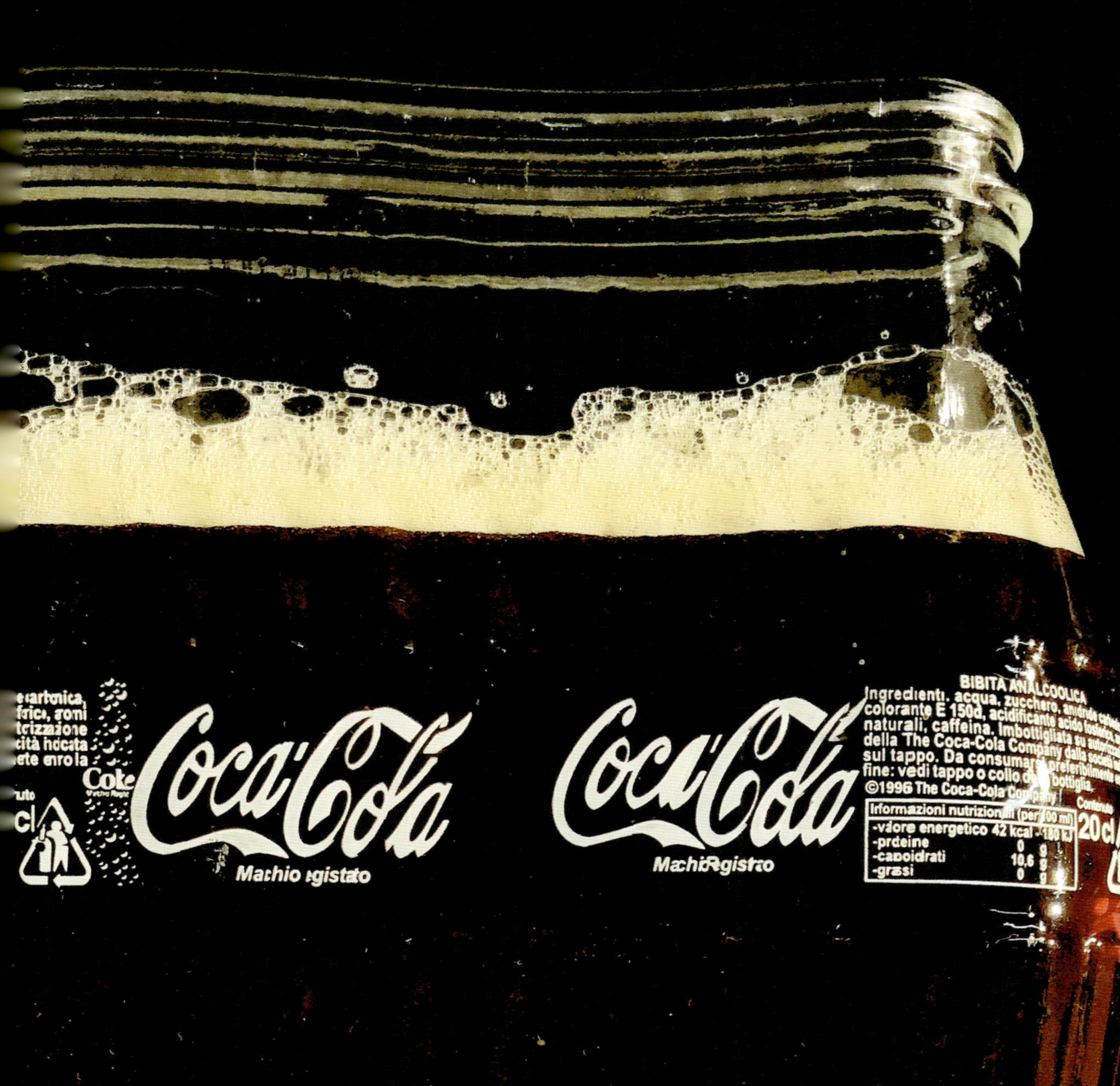
Coca-Cola
Marchio registrato
Coca-Cola
Marchio Registrato
Coke
BIBITA ANALCOOLICA
Ingredienti. acqua, zucchero, anidride carbonica,
colorante E 150d, acidificante acido fosforico, aromi
naturali, caffeina. Imbottigliata su autorizzazione
della The Coca-Cola Company dalla società indicata
sul tappo. Da consumarsi preferibilmente entro la
fine: vedi tappo o collo della bottiglia.
©1996 The Coca-Cola Company
Informazioni nutrizionali (per 100 ml)
-valore energetico 42 kcal - 180 kJ
-proteine 0 g
-carboidrati 10,6 g
-grassi 0 g
Contenuto 20 cl

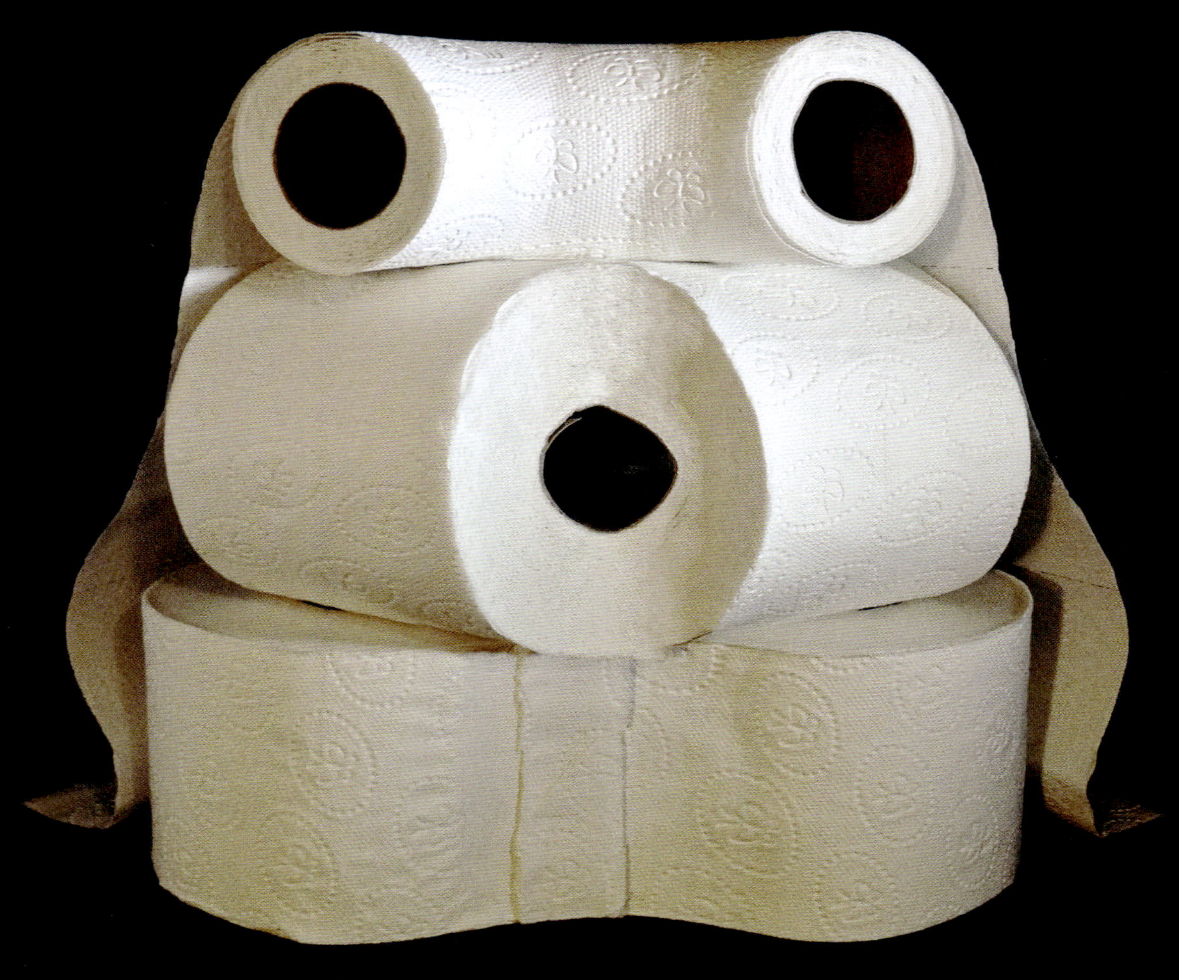

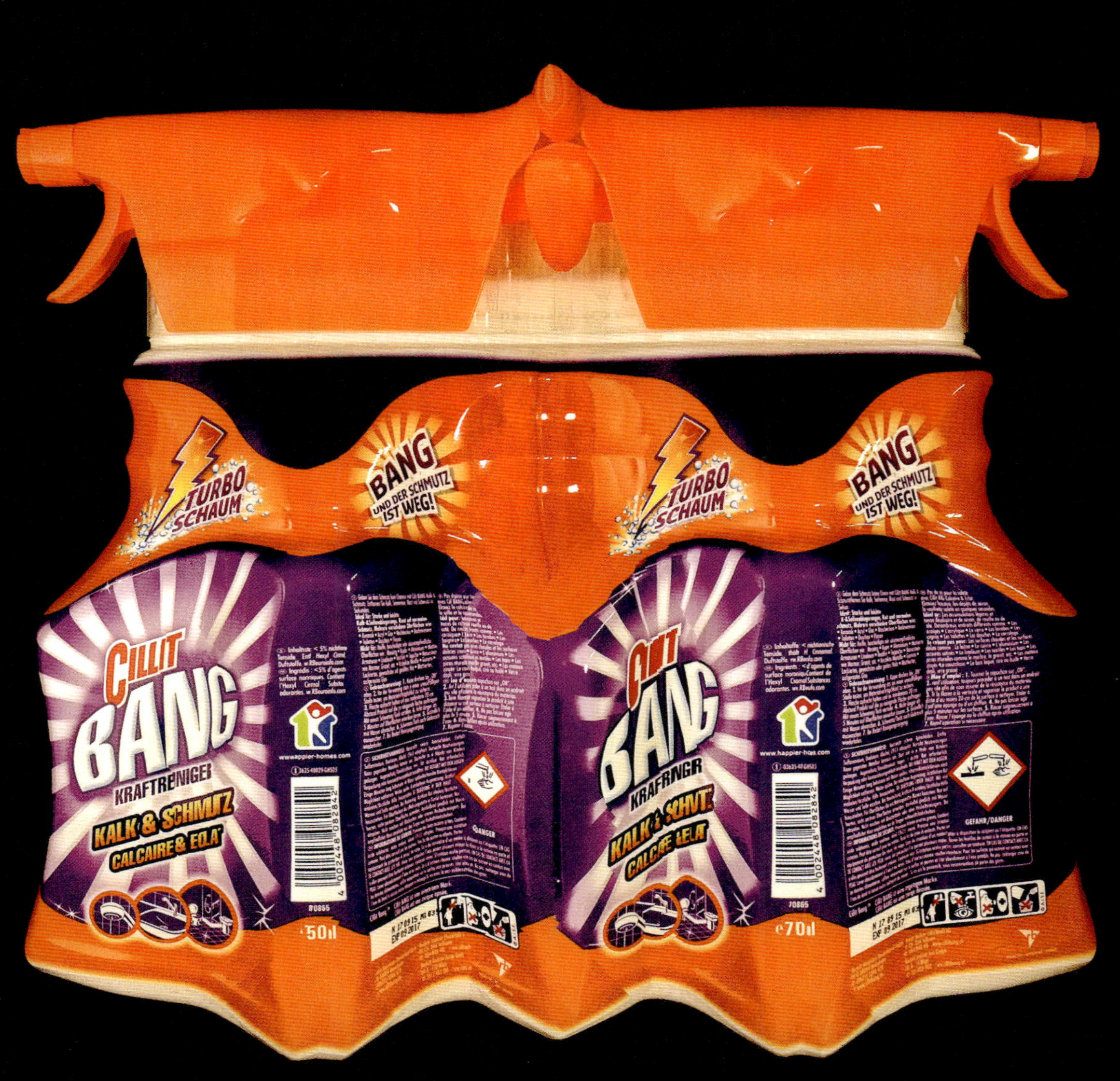

TURBO SCHAUM
BANG UND DER SCHMUTZ IST WEG!
TURBO SCHAUM
BANG UND DER SCHMUTZ IST WEG!
CILLIT
BANG
KRAFTREINIGER
KALK & SCHMUTZ
CALCAIRE & SOLA'
www.happier-homes.com
50ml
BANG
KRAFRNGR
KALK & SCHVT.
CALCAIRE & LEUT
www.happier-hlas.com
70ml
GEFAHR/DANGER

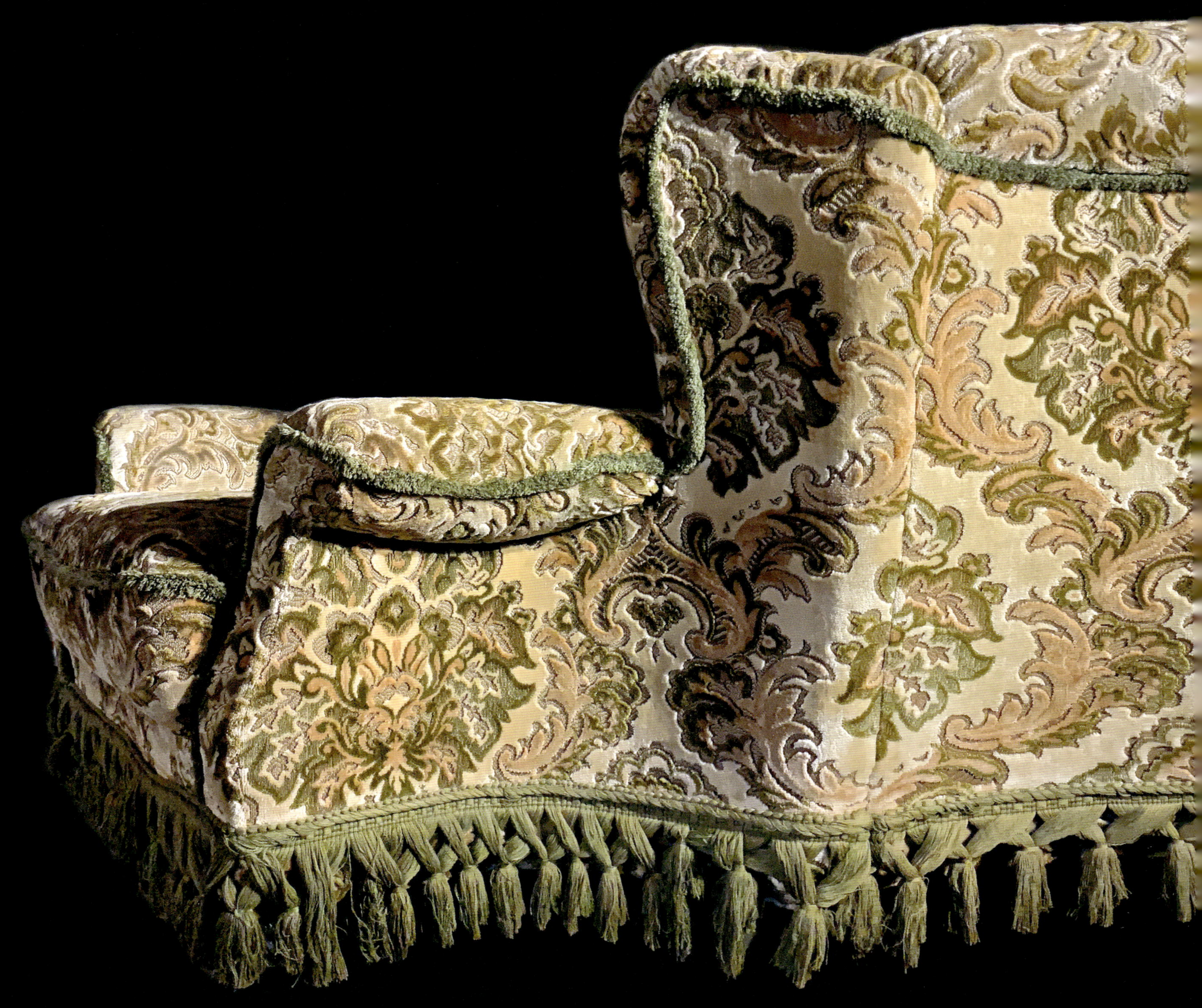

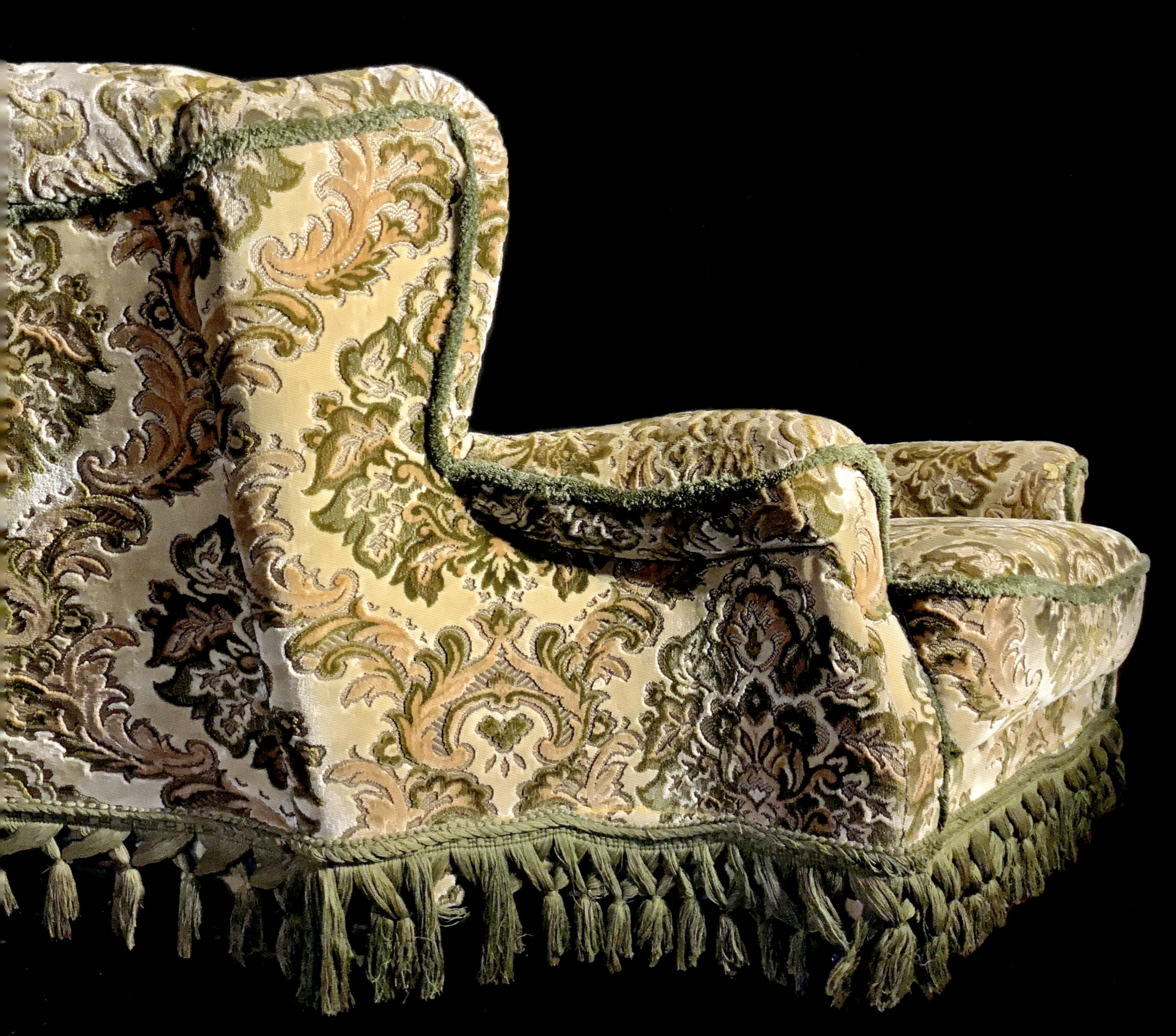

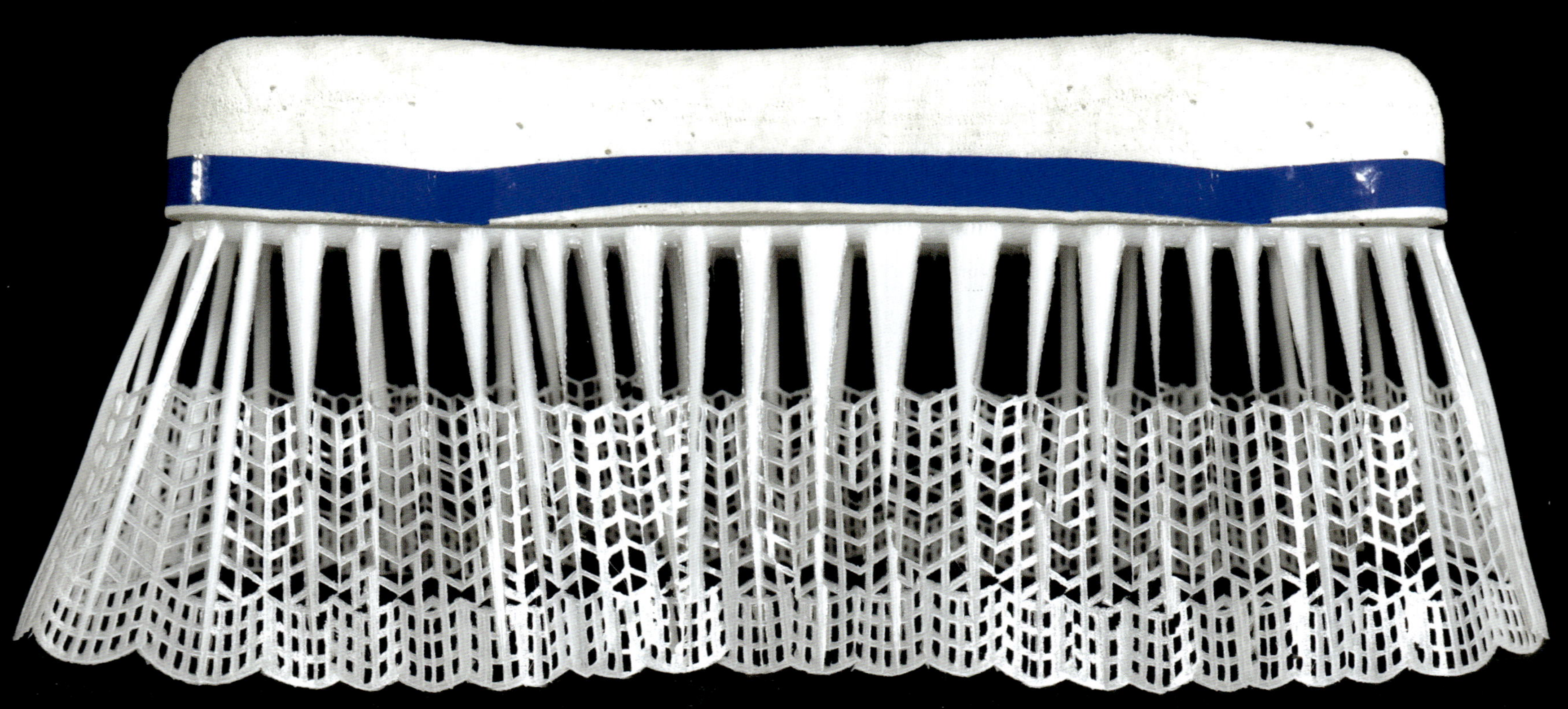

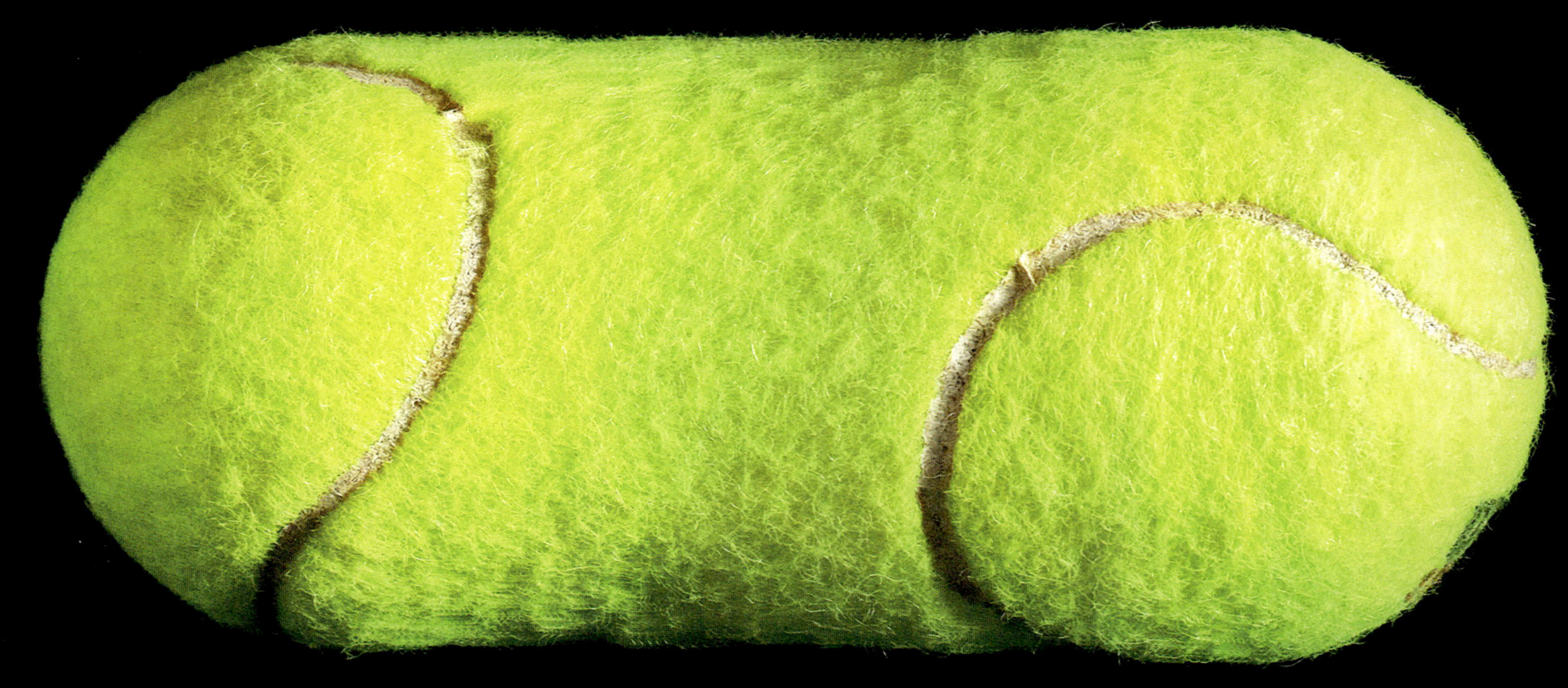

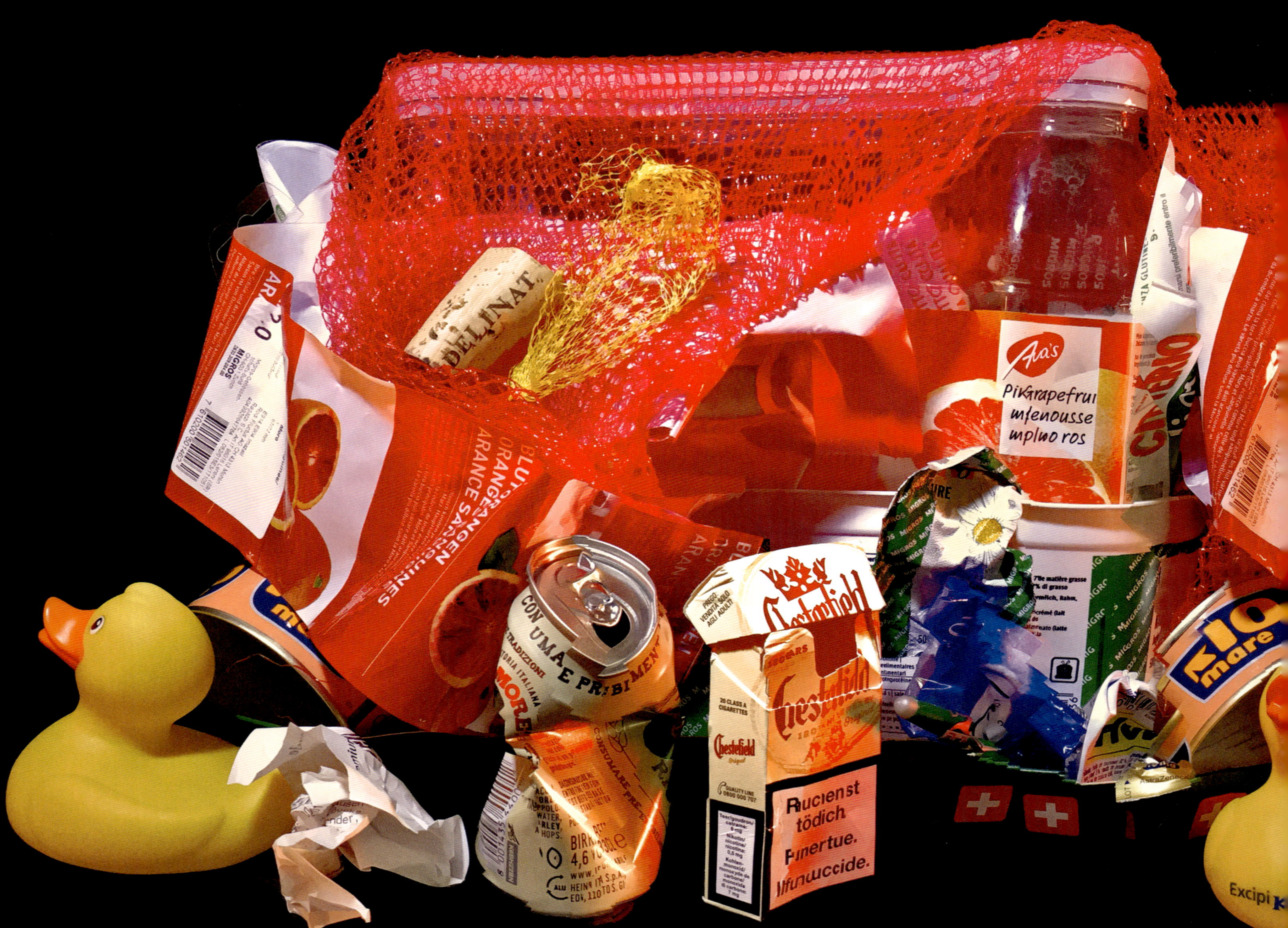

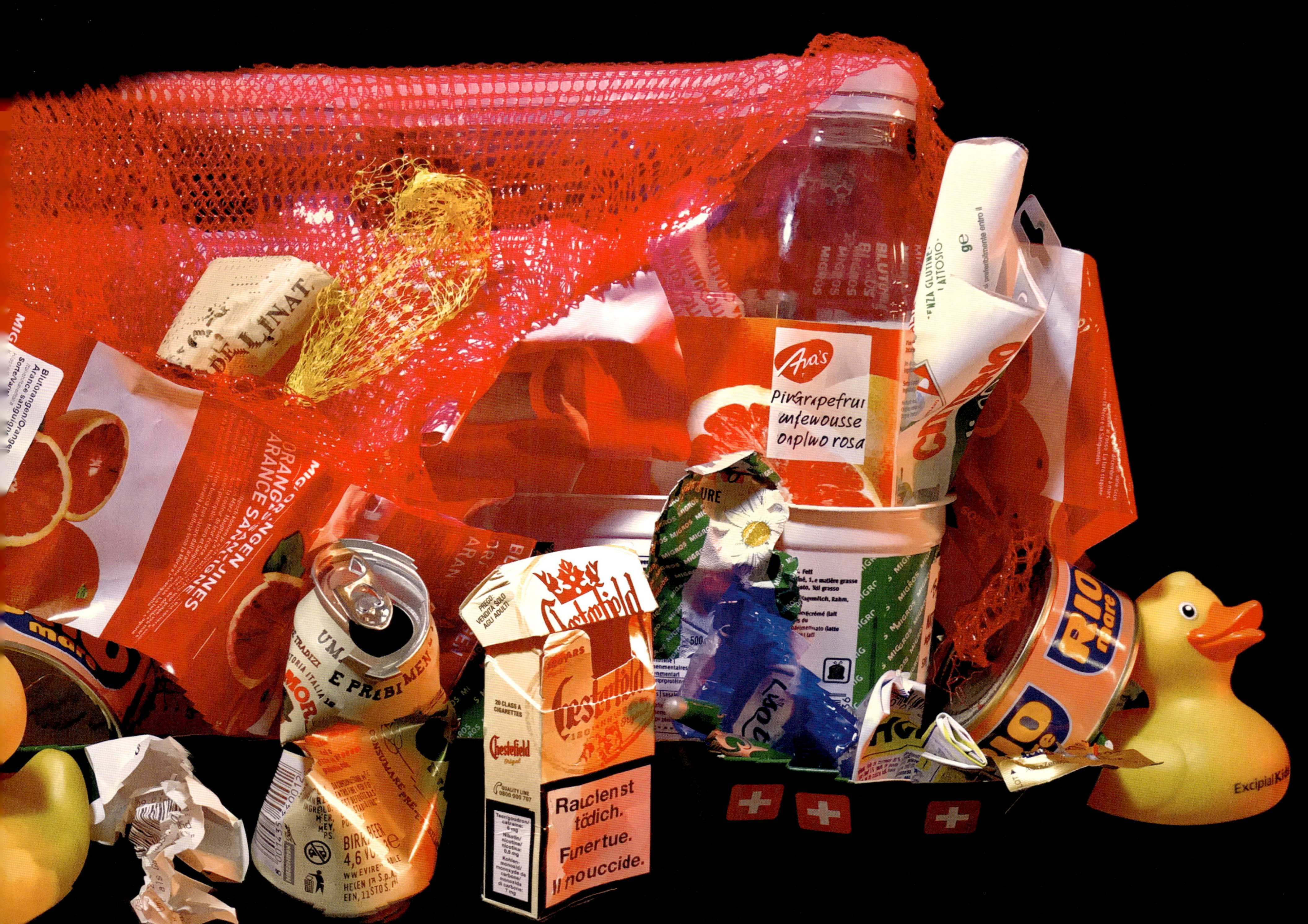

Blutorangen/Orange
Arancia sanguigna/Orange
sortey
MIG
ORANG
ARANCI
SANGEN
ORANGE
ARANCE SANGUIGNES
Ara's
PinGrapefrui
enfewousse
onpiwo rosa
Chesterfield
20 CLASS A
CIGARETTES
Chesterfield
Original
QUALITY LINE
0800 000 707
Rauchen ist
tödlich.
Fumer tue.
Il nuoccide.
Teergehalt/goudron:
6 mg
Nikotin/
nicotine/
nicotina:
0,5 mg
Kohlen-
monoxyd/
monoxyde de
carbone/
monossido
di carbonio:
7 mg
RIO
RIO
Excipial Kids
UM
E PREBI MEN
VITTORIA ITALIA
CONSUMARE PRE
BIRK BEER
4,6 vo
WWEVIRE
HEIEN IR S.P.A.
EEN, 11STO S. M
PREZZO
VENDITA SOLO
AGLI ADULTI
500
MIGROS
URE
ge

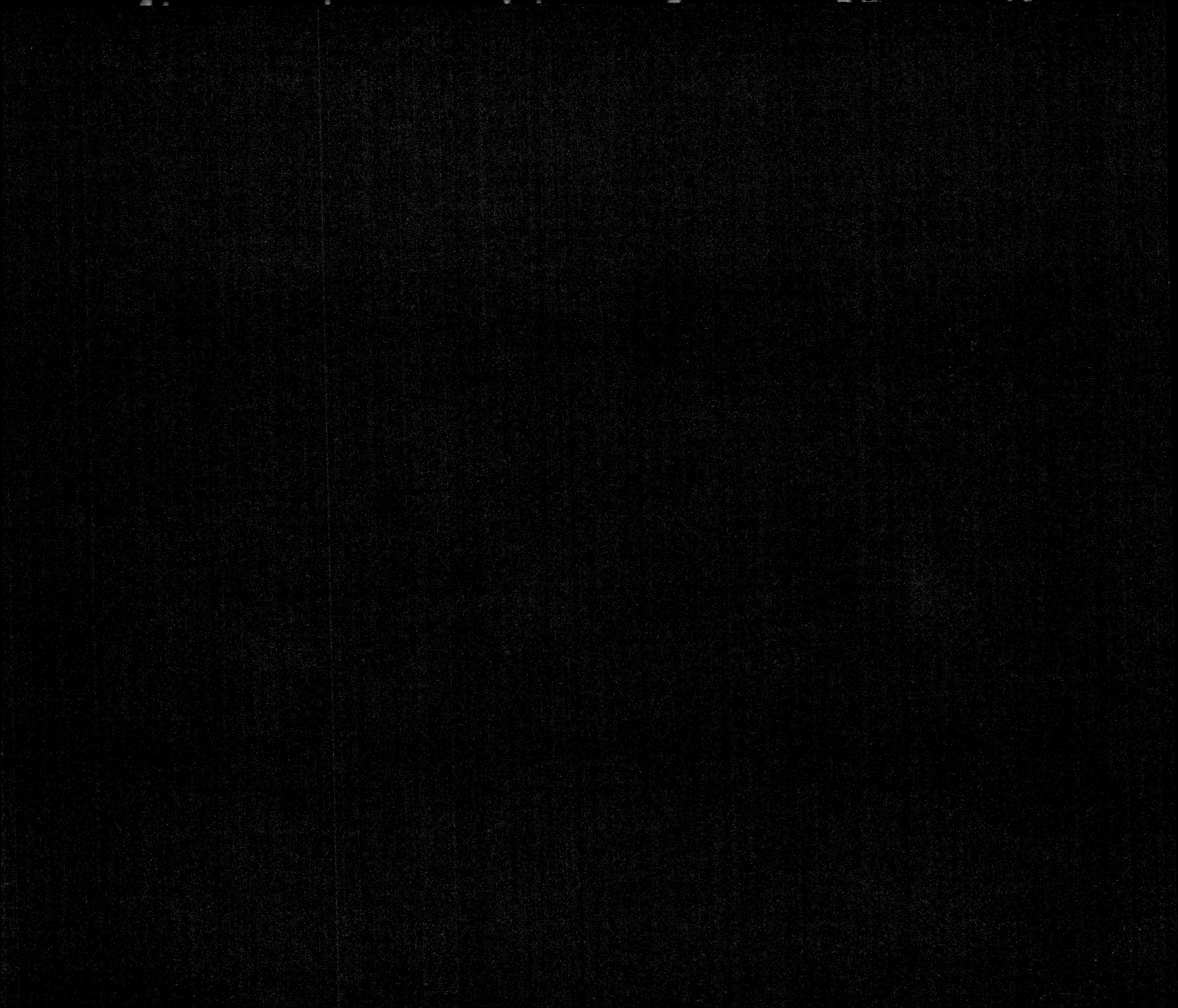

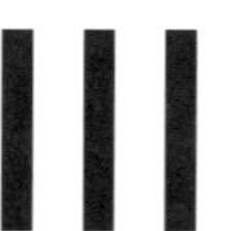

ROTO LABORATORY

OTO LABORATORY R

TO LABORATORY RO

O LABORATORY ROT

LABORATORY ROTO

# ROTATIONS

When the surface of an object can be easily removed and
flattened as the label on a tin can (cf. fig. above right),
then there are no secrets left which cannot be revealed!
A cylindrical object has a rectangular, quasi two-
dimensional surface, just like a label has. Therefore,
a two-dimensional image of a tin could in theory be
generated by rolling it along the screen of a photocopier,
though this has so far not led to satisfactory results.
But what happens to an orange?
Here, the detached peel becomes a new, three-
dimensionally folded structure (bottom right). As a result,
the unrolling image – the rotography – is an abstraction.
A kind of "one-frame-movie" is developed, as if an orange
were rolling across the table in front of us and we could
track the image with our eye.
The panorama technique of digital cameras is based on
a panning motion. First, a normal image is recorded, and
this is then – with a left to right motion – extended and
widened in the right half of the image by adding a series of
narrow, vertical image strips.
Once the recording is complete, the camera software
processes the images and stitches them into a contiguous
whole.
It is particularly important that the image parts fit
together precisely during this process, and that any small
distortions or color changes at the seams are corrected as
far as possible. In fact, the panorama function can be used
to photograph not only static, but also rotating objects,
thereby serving as the key to a fascinating new world of
roll-off images, rotography.



# ABROLLBILDER



*Wenn man die Oberfläche eines Objekts so einfach
ablösen und ausbreiten kann wie das Etikett einer Konservendose (Pelati, vgl. Abb. rechts oben), gibt es kaum
Geheimnisse und Überraschungen:*
*Ein zylindrisches Objekt hat eine rechteckige, quasi zweidi-
mensionale Oberfläche, so wie dieses Etikett. Ein entspre-
chendes Abrollbild der Konservendose könnte auch
erzeugt werden, indem man diese über einen Photokopierer
rollen lässt. Das führt aber nicht zu befriedigenden
Resultaten.*
*Was aber passiert mit der Orange?*
*Hier wird die abgelöste Schale zu einer neuen, dreidimen-
sional verfalteten Struktur (rechts unten). Das Abrollbild
indessen – die Rotographie – ist eine Abstraktion. Als ob
eine Orange vor uns über den Tisch rollen würde und wir
das Bild so im Auge behalten könnten, eine Art „one-frame-
movie".*
*Die Panoramatechnik der Digitalkameras beruht auf einer
Schwenkbewegung. Dabei wird zuerst ein normales Bild
aufgezeichnet, welches sodann – bei einer Bewegungsrich-
tung von links nach rechts – in der rechten Bildhälfte durch
schmale, vertikale Bildstreifen ergänzt und verbreitert wird.
Wenn der Aufnahmeprozess abgeschlossen ist, folgt die
Verarbeitung, die Kamerasoftware fügt das Bild zu einem
Ganzen. Dabei ist von besonderer Bedeutung, dass bei
diesem Vorgang die Bildteile passgenau aneinander gefügt
sowie kleine Verzerrungen und Farbänderungen an den
Nahtstellen soweit möglich ausgeglichen werden.*
*Dass sich die Panoramafunktion auch dazu benutzen lässt,
ein drehendes Objekt so aufzunehmen, dass ein Abrollbild
entsteht, ist verblüffend und war der Schlüssel zu dieser
neuen Bildwelt, der Rotographie.*

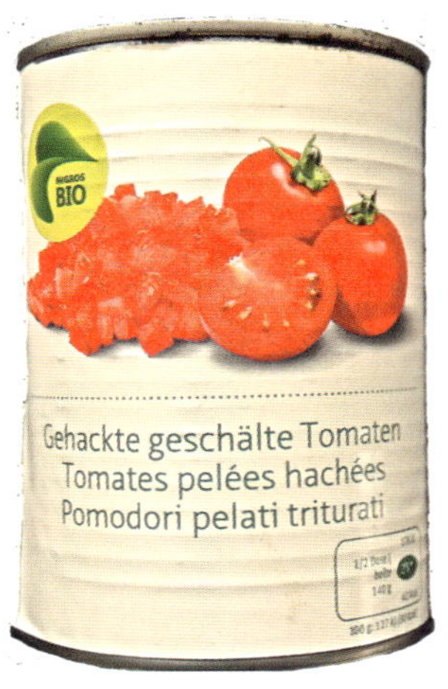


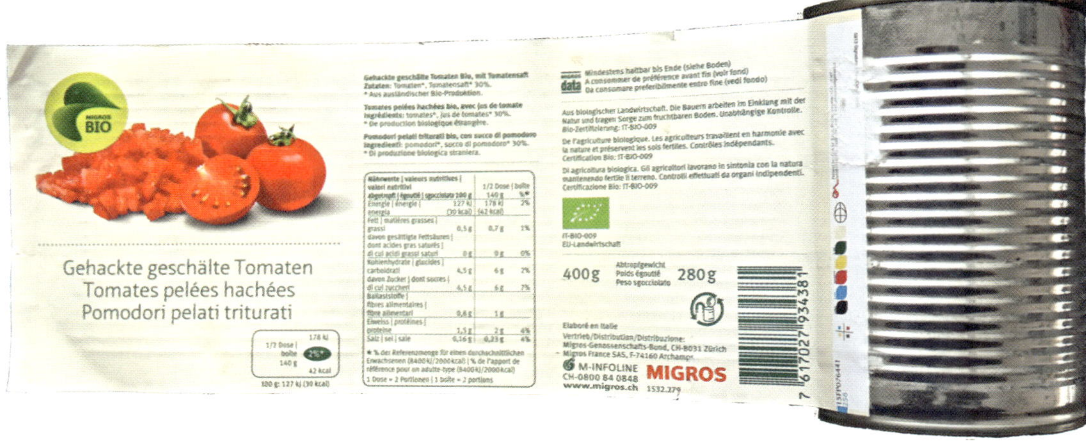


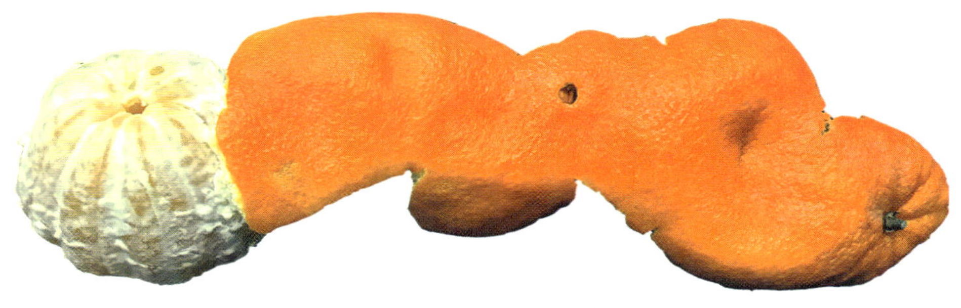

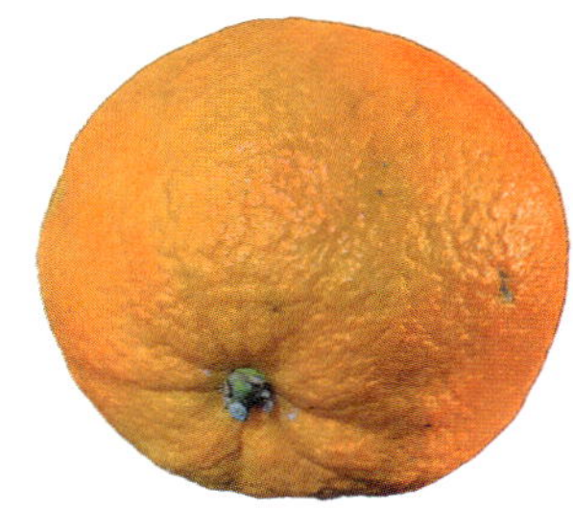

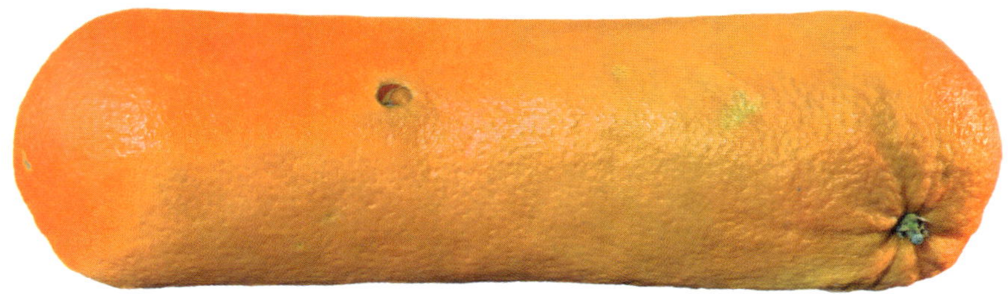

(oben links) Konservendose und abgerolltes Etikett;
(unten) Orange in normaler Ansicht, mit abgeschälter Schale
und als Rotographie um rund 270° abgedreht.

(top) Canned food in normal view and with the label peeled off;
(bottom) Orange, normal view, with the peeled off peel, and as
rotography rotated by about 270°.

# STUDIES

Unrolled images of natural objects show us how readily the identity of an object is revealed through its surface structure and color, even when the shape is completely transformed.

The spherical melon (right) becomes cylindrical, the characteristic meridional markings of its skin are still visible. These markings become waves or sinusoidal curves. The superimposition of a characteristically irregular, fractal network is intriguing. This network is formed by a cork-like bark tissue (callus), which closes the cracks which occur when the melon is growing.

The patterns in the skin of the melon allow it to remain recognizable, even in its new form. While still familiar to us, the unrolled images delight us with their subtle abstraction and new aesthetic.

This kind of illustration (example p. 32/33) harks back to the work of Ernst Haeckel ("Kunstformen der Natur", Verlag des Bibliographischen Instituts, Leipzig and Vienna, 1904) as well as to that of Karl Blossfeldt. Due to Blossfeldt's iconic, aesthetic, black and white photographs, interest in botany-based art underwent something of a renaissance a hundred years ago (Karl Blossfeldt, "Urformen der Kunst", Wasmuth, Berlin, 1928). As a tribute to his work, one such botanical image is shown on pages 28/29. The subject matter is the remains of a pumpkin plant, the neck of the root. What is revealed is the transition between the plant's bulbous roots and the highly filigreed vascular system which connects to the stalks and leaves.



# STUDIEN

*Abrollbilder biologischer Objekte offenbaren die Ausdruckskraft ihrer Struktur in ganz besonderem Masse. Es tritt eine neue Körperlichkeit hervor, die von der vertrauten Gegenständlichkeit losgelöst ist.*

*Aus der kugelförmigen Melone (rechts) wird eine rundliche Walze, ihre Rinde ist gezeichnet von den meridionalen Schnitzspuren ihres Grundaufbaus. Diese regelmässigen Formen zeichnen sich als Wellen oder sinusartige Kurven ab. Spannend ist die Überlagerung durch ein charakteristisch unregelmässiges, fraktales Netz. Dieses besteht aus korkartigem Rindengewebe (Kallus), welches die Wachstumsrisse verschliesst. Allein kraft ihrer Oberflächenstruktur, die sich durch Wiederholung akzentuiert, werden die Objekte auf eine neue Art les- und erkennbar. Sie sind uns vertraut, überraschen uns aber mit einer subtilen Abstraktivität und Ästhetik.*

*Diese Art der Abbildung (Beispiel S. 32/33) nimmt auch Bezug auf die Arbeiten von Ernst Haeckel („Kunstformen der Natur", Verlag des Bibliographischen Instituts, Leipzig und Wien, 1904) sowie auf Karl Blossfeldt, der vor hundert Jahren das visuell Überraschende der Gestalt von Pflanzen mit seinen reduzierten, hyper-ästhetischen Schwarzweissphotographien herausarbeitete (Karl Blossfeldt, „Urformen der Kunst", Wasmuth, Berlin, 1928). Als Hommage an seine Abbildungstechnik ist auf den Seiten 28/29 ein solches Objekt abgebildet. Es handelt sich um das Relikt einer Kürbispflanze, den Wurzelhals.*

*Was sich offenbart ist der Architekturwechsel der Pflanze zwischen dem knolligen Wurzelbereich und den filigranen, hochgeordneten Leitstrukturen an der Basis des oberirdischen Sprossteils mit den Verzweigungen zu den Blattstengeln.*

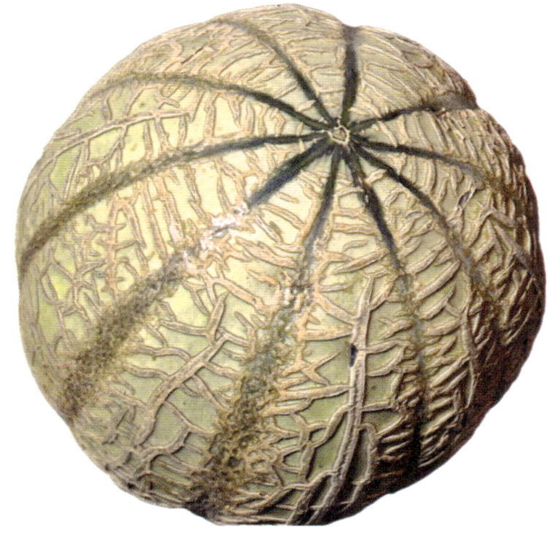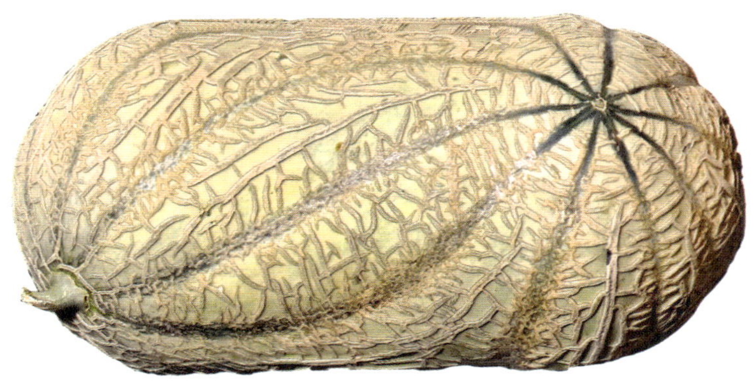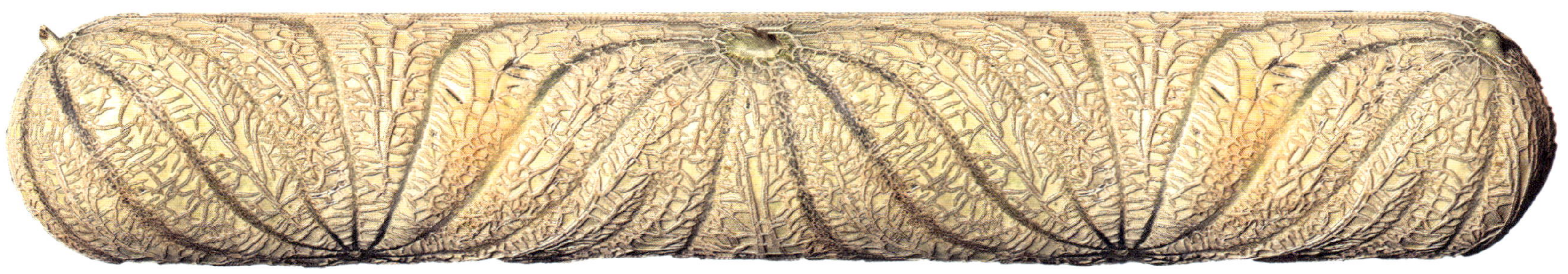

Studien an einer Melone (Cavaillon): Ansicht (oben links); Kurz-Ro-tographie, Umdrehung um 90° (oben rechts); sowie als Rotographie über mehrere Umdrehungen (630°) (unten).

Studies on a melon (Cavaillon): normal view (top left); roto-graphs: rotation by 90° (top right); and over several rotations (630°) (bottom).

# GEOMETRY

The unusually shaped cheese packaging shown as an example on the right illustrates some of the fundamental principles of rotographic imaging.
The basic shape is a truncated pyramid (top left). The simple rotation as a rotography (bottom left) results in the sides of the horizontal surfaces (top and bottom) being rendered curved, like a segment of a circle. In contrast, the verticals (or the steep sides of the pyramid) remain straight lines.
Similarly, this is visible in the "somersault" image (right) – i.e. when rotating around a horizontal axis: the horizontal lines remain straight, the pyramid base is folded up in a round shape.
By rotating an object on the turntable of a gramophone by 90° to 180° in front of a camera fixed on a tripod, it is possible to record the image as if simultaneously from two or more sides. A new object emerges and the perspective dissapears.

What is alluded to here is Cubism with its decomposition of the form of an object into a so-called "multiview". The most well-known are the ingenious depictions of violins and guitars in the paintings of Picasso, Braque and Gris.

# GEOMETRIE

*An der rechts als Beispiel abgebildeten, charakteristisch geformten Käseverpackung lassen sich einige Grundprinzipien der Rotographie-Abbildung aufzeigen:*
*Die Grundform ist ein Pyramidenstumpf (oben links). Die einfache Drehung als Rotographie (unten links) führt dazu, dass die Seiten der horizontalen Flächen (Ober- und Unterseite) gebogen, als Kreissegment, wiedergegeben werden. Demgegenüber bleiben die Vertikalen (bzw. die steilen Pyramidenseiten) als Geraden erhalten.*
*Analog ist dies bei der „Purzelbaum"-Aufnahme (rechts), d. h. bei der Drehung um eine horizontale Achse sichtbar: Die horizontalen Linien bleiben gerade, die Pyramidengrundfläche wird rund eingefaltet.*
*Mit der besonderen Aufnahmetechnik, vor der auf einem Stativ fixierten Kamera einen Gegenstand auf dem Plattenteller eines alten Grammophons um 90° bis 180° abzudrehen, gelingt es, das Objekt quasi gleichzeitig von zwei oder mehreren Seiten abzubilden: Es entsteht ein neuer Körper, die Perspektive löst sich auf.*

*Was hier anklingt ist der Kubismus mit seiner Zerlegung der Form eines Gegenstandes in eine sogenannte „Mehransichtigkeit". Berühmt sind die genialen mehransichtigen Kompositionen der klassischen Objekte Violine oder Gitarre in den Bildern von Picasso, Braque und Gris.*

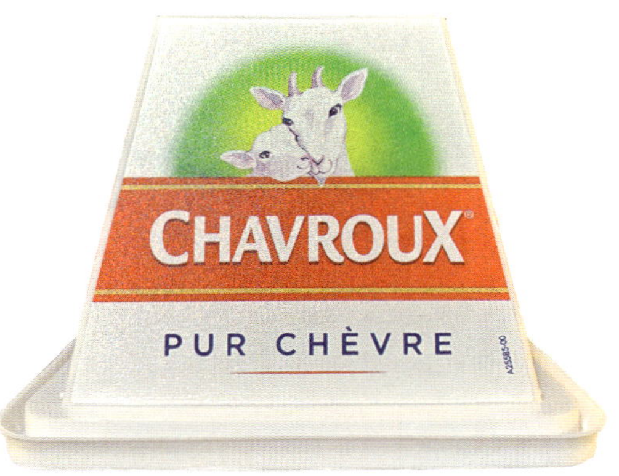

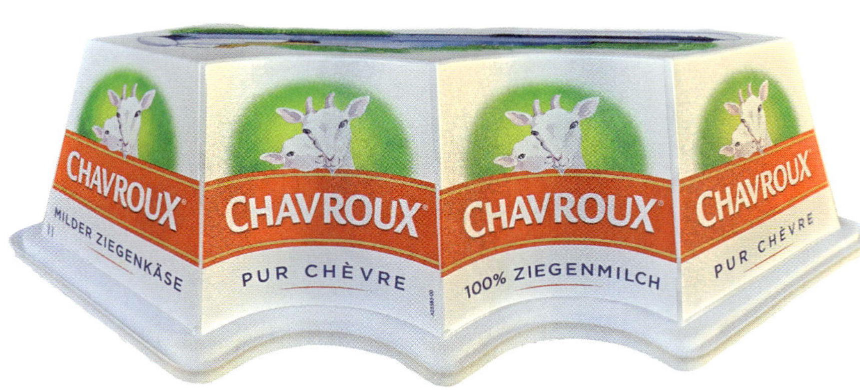

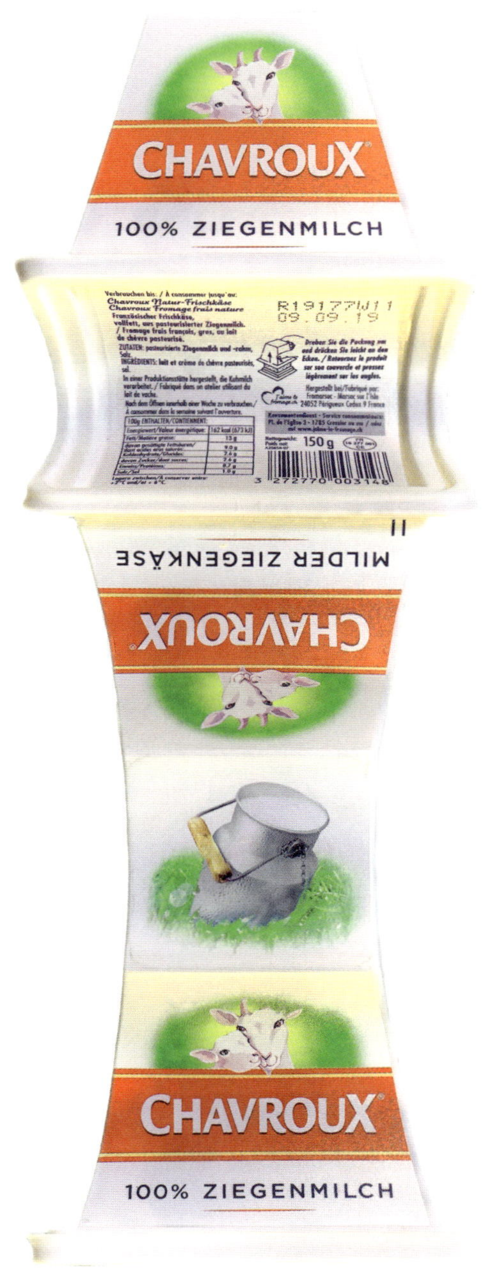

Rotographiestudie Käseverpackung „Chavroux", Einzelansicht; horizontale und vertikale Abwicklung, vgl. Text links.

Rotography study "Chavroux" cheese packaging, single view; horizontal and vertical unrolling, cf. text on the left.

# PORTRAITS



# PORTRAITS



The human head lends itself to experiments in multiple representations of the face. A classic example is the Roman god Janus, the Two-Faced, a two-faced head featuring four eyes and two noses.

The same type of representation is also found – presumably originating independently – in several other cultures. For example, page 72 shows a two-faced mask from Africa (Congo; Museum Rietberg, Zurich, 2019). An even more complex example is the sculptural altar figure (left). The hemispherical head has three faces, each sharing one eye, i.e., there are four eyes and three noses. The same structure also appears in the caricature drawing by H. Daumier (right).

Another outcome of rotographic composition is that inanimate objects can appear as faces e.g. as shown in the picture "Lemon" (p. 53). New, surprising body shapes can be created in rotographies of pieces of wood. For example, in the rotography of a sawn branch (p. 60), the bust of a female figure emerges (p. 61). And the dead trunk of a clematis (p. 54/55) is transformed into a completely new sculpture; a row of male torsos clad in armor.

*Der Kopf des Menschen bietet sich an für Experimente, mehrere Gesichter darzustellen. Klassisch und sprichwörtlich ist der römische Janus, der Zwiespältige, ein doppelgesichtiger Kopf mit vier Augen und zwei Nasen.*

*Dieselbe Art der Darstellung findet sich auch – vermutlich unabhängig entstanden – in ganz unterschiedlichen Kulturen: Als Beispiel ist auf Seite 72 eine zweigesichtige afrikanische Maske wiedergegeben (Kongo; Museum Rietberg, Zürich, 2019).*
*Komplexer ist die skulpturale Altarfigur (links): Der halbkugelförmige Kopf hat drei Gesichter, die sich je ein Auge teilen, d. h. vier Augen und drei Nasen. Denselben Aufbau hat auch die Karikaturzeichnung von H. Daumier (rechts).*

*Ein weiteres spannendes Feld ist die rotographische Komposition von Gesichtern, wie sie zum Beispiel im Bild „Zitrone" (S. 53) aufscheint. Neue, überraschende Körperformen entstehen in den Rotographien z. B. von Holzstücken: In der Rotographie eines angesägten Astholzes (S. 60) tritt die Büste einer Frauenfigur hervor (S. 61). Und das trockene Stammholz einer Waldrebe (S. 54/55) fügt sich zu einer ganz neuen Skulptur: zu einem drei- und fünffachen Männertorso.*

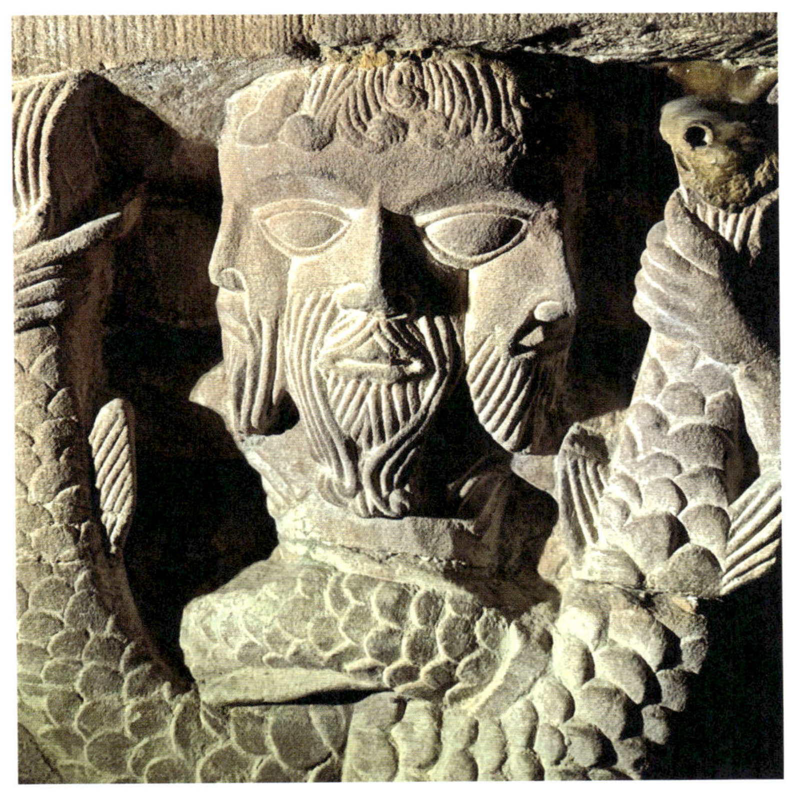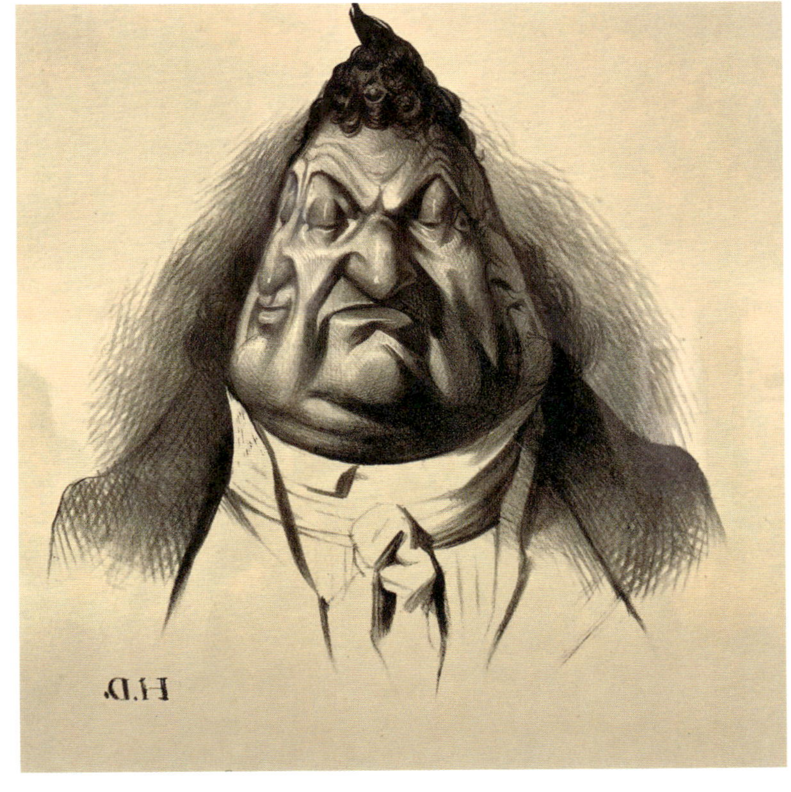

(links) Dreigesicht, Figur an der Basis eines Altars im Basler Mün-
ster (Sandstein, Aufnahme 2019); (rechts)„Die Vergangenheit, Die
Gegenwart, Die Zukunft" (1834), Karikatur von Honoré Daumier.

(left) Three-face, figure at the base of an altar in the Cathedral
of Basel (sandstone, photo 2019); (right) "The Past, The Present,
The Future" (1834), caricature by Honoré Daumier.

# LABORATORY

A rotating object can be recorded in such a way that a continuous rolling image is created; a rotography. In order to do this, one needs a camera with a panorama mode, fixed on a tripod, in front of which an object rotates on a turntable.
The idea, the initial attempt and – eureka – the first convincing results sent me into a frenzy back in January 2013 and inspired a fascination and enthusiasm which continue to this day.
I soon realized that the panorama function of a digital camera could produce an image even if only part of the object field was undergoing directional movement.
The quality of my first attempts was not satisfactory because the objects rotated too fast. This was remedied by adjusting the speed of the turntable.
For small rotation angles (e.g. for the images "Shoe" on page 68 or "Colander" on page 65), the turntable is rotated slowly approx. 90° by hand. For rotographies like "Brick" (p. 58/59), a slow, steady drive was very useful, since the exposure took about six minutes over five complete revolutions.
A further improvement was achieved by experimenting with the lighting. For most objects, soft lighting against a black background produces the best results.
My rotographies are created with a multitude of digital cameras as well as iPhone inbuilt cameras.



# ROTOSKOP

*Ein sich drehendes Objekt kann so aufgenommen werden, dass ein kontinuierliches Abrollbild entsteht, eine Rotographie. Dazu geeignet ist eine auf einem Stativ fixierte Kamera mit Panoramamodus, vor der sich ein Objekt dreht, zum Beispiel auf dem Plattenteller eines Grammophons.*

*Die Idee, der initiale Versuch und – Heureka – das erste überzeugende Resultat haben mich damals (am 2. Januar 2013) in einen Rausch versetzt, eine inspirierende, faszinierende Trance, eine Begeisterung, die bis heute anhält.*

*Die notwendige Ausrüstung ist überraschend einfach, sie besteht aus einem Stativ und einer drehbaren Unterlage. Ich habe diese mit einfachsten Mitteln aufgebaut, als mir klar geworden war, dass die Panoramafunktion der Digitalkamera unter bestimmten Umständen auch dann ein Bild erzeugt und – durch Stitching – fortsetzt, wenn nur ein Teil des Objektfeldes eine gerichtete Bewegung erfährt.*

*Die Qualität war in diesen ersten Versuchen nicht befriedigend, da sich die Objekte zu rasch drehten. Dies liess sich beheben, indem die Untersetzung des Plattenspielers angepasst wurde. Für geringe Drehwinkel (z. B. bei den Aufnahmen „Schuh", S. 68, oder „Sieb", S. 65) wird der Plattenteller ohne Antrieb langsam um ca. 90° gedreht. Für Rotographien wie „Ziegelstein" (S. 58/59) ist der langsame, gleichmässige Antrieb sehr dienlich, da die Aufnahme über fünf ganze Umdrehungen rund sechs Minuten dauerte.*
*Eine wichtige Optimierung wurde erreicht durch das Experimentieren mit der Beleuchtung. Bei den meisten Objekten führt eine weiche Ausleuchtung vor schwarzem Hintergrund zu guten Resultaten. Für die Rotographien wurden verschiedene digitale Kameras und iPhone-Typen genutzt.*

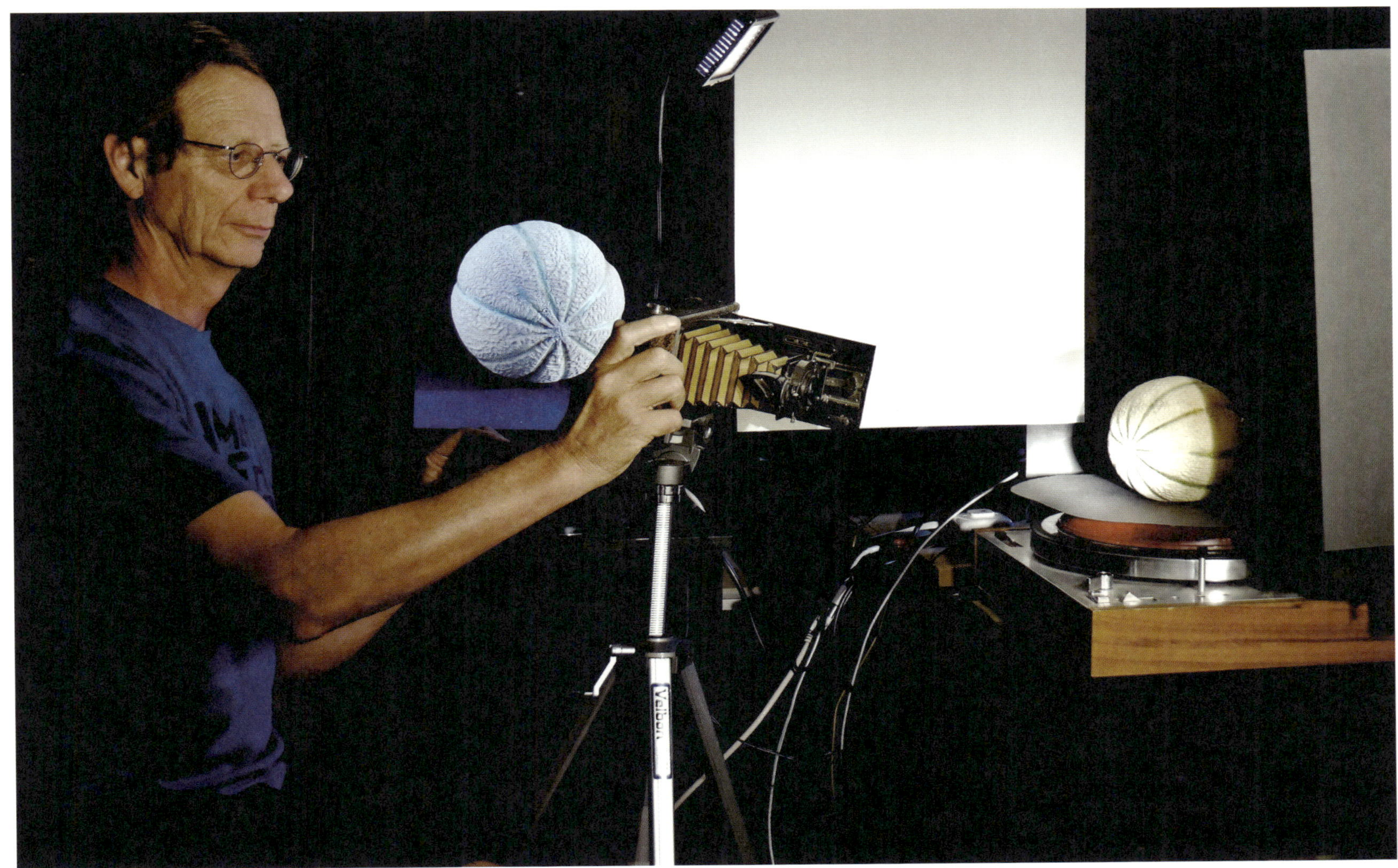

Anordnung mit Plattenspieler, Kamera und Stativ. Das Objekt dreht sich auf dem Plattenspieler vor schwarzem Hintergrund, ausgeleuchtet durch Spots (in Bildrichtung). Die Kamera ist auf einem Stativ fixiert. Dahinter sind ein Reflektor und ein Kontrollbildschirm angeordnet.

Arrangement with turntable, camera and tripod. The object rotates on a turntable in front of a black background, illuminated by spots pointing in the direction of the image. The camera is fixed on a tripod. Behind it are a reflector and a control screen.

# ABSTRACT

The panoramic function of digital cameras allows the capture of images with an elongated field of vision.
It also enables one to take a picture while circling round an object or while the object ist turning. This technique depicts multiple concurrent perspectives of the object, creating a rotography.
In rotographies, the normal perspective is lost and objects appear more abstract as a result, reminiscent of cubistic works of art. The objects are often not immediately recognizable and hence leave the viewer plenty of room for imagination and optical illusion.

# ABSTRACT

*Die Panoramafunktion von Digitalkameras ermöglicht es, Bilder über ein verlängertes Sichtfeld aufzunehmen.
Es erweist sich auch als gangbar, ein Bild aufzunehmen, während wir ein Objekt umkreisen beziehungsweise ein drehendes Objekt von einem Punkt aus aufzunehmen.
Diese Technik führt zu Aufnahmen, welche aufeinanderfolgende Blickwinkel auf das Objekt kontinuierlich zusammenhängen. Dadurch wird eine Abwicklung der Oberflächengestalt erzeugt – ein Abrollbild, eine Rotographie.
In den Rotographien ist die Perspektive auf eigentümliche Art aufgehoben und die Objekte erscheinen als abstrakte Artefakte. Obwohl sofort erkennbar, sind sie in einen Raum von Phantasie und Illusion entrückt und weisen Anklänge an kubistische Kunstwerke auf.*

# AUTOR

*Jürg Stünzi (1954) lebt in Thalwil (Schweiz), ist verheiratet und Vater von drei erwachsenen Kindern. Seit seinem Jugendalter beschäftigt er sich mit Photographie. Im Studium der Naturwissenschaften (Biologie, Dr. phil. II) eignete er sich den professionellen Zugang zur Mikro- und Makrophotographie an sowie zur Dunkelkammertechnik. Fasziniert von den kreativen Möglichkeiten der Digitalphotographie erschliesst er sich heute verschiedenste Felder experimenteller Abbildungstechniken, insbesondere mit den Spielarten der Panoramafunktionen.*

*Jürg Stünzi ist in diversen Kunstprojekten engagiert. Seit der ersten Einzelausstellung seiner photographischen Arbeiten (KOLTAI MAURER, Zürich, 25.5.–2.6.2013) präsentierte er seine Werke in weiteren sechs Ausstellungen.*

# AUTHOR

Jürg Stünzi (1954) lives in Thalwil, Switzerland, is married and father to three adult children. He has had a keen interest in photography since his youth. During his doctorate in Biology, he developed a professional approach to micro- and macrophotography as well as to darkroom techniques. Fascinated by the creative possibilities of digital photography, he is now exploring various fields of experimental imaging techniques, especially those using panorama functions.

Jürg Stünzi is involved in many art projects. Since his first solo exhibition of photographic works (KOLTAI MAURER, Zurich, 25.5.–2.6.2013) he has presented his works in six further exhibitions.

# THANKS

I would like to offer my heartfelt thanks to all those who have contributed to the creation of this book. I would especially like to mention the support of Sebastian Ernst, who created the graphic concept and contributed a great deal to the design of the book. For the review of images and texts I would like to thank Verena Eichenberger, Simone Stünzi and Susan Bryant. Discussion and translation of the texts was done by Sue Jennings. My thanks also go to Markus Braun, who positively took up my book project and included it in his publishing program. The realization of the book could only take place thanks to generous financial support in the form of production cost contributions by the following institutions:
Gemeinde Thalwil; Fachstelle Kultur
Bank Raiffeisen, Thalwil
Bank Thalwil, Thalwil

# DANKSAGUNG

*Ich danke allen, die zum Entstehen dieses Buches beigetragen haben. Ganz besonders hervorheben möchte ich die Unterstützung von Sebastian Ernst, der das graphische Konzept geschaffen und sehr viel zur Gestaltung des Buches beigetragen hat. Für die Durchsicht von Bildern und Texten danke ich Verena Eichenberger, Simone Stünzi und Susan Bryant. Die Diskussion und Übersetzung der Texte erfolgte durch Sue Jennings.*
*Mein Dank geht auch an Markus Braun, der mein Buchprojekt positiv aufgriff und in sein Verlagsprogramm aufgenommen hat. Die Realisierung des Buches konnte nur dank grosszügiger finanzieller Unterstützung in Form von Produktionskostenbeiträgen durch die folgenden Institutionen erfolgen:*
*Gemeinde Thalwil; Fachstelle Kultur*
*Bank Raiffeisen, Thalwil*
*Bank Thalwil, Thalwil*

**ROTO** APPENDIX

**OTO** APPENDIX**R**

**TO** APPENDIX**RO**

**O** APPENDIX**ROT**

APPENDIX**ROTO**

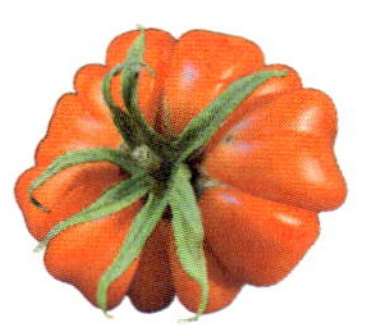 p. 26/27
**Tomato**
- Tomate
Revolution 360°
2019-09-06

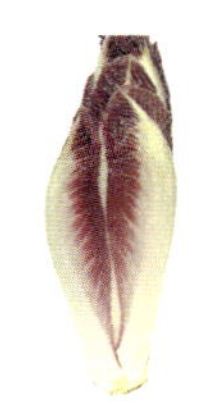 p. 36
**Chiccorino rosso trevisano**
- Trevisan
2 ½ Revolutions
2017-04-22

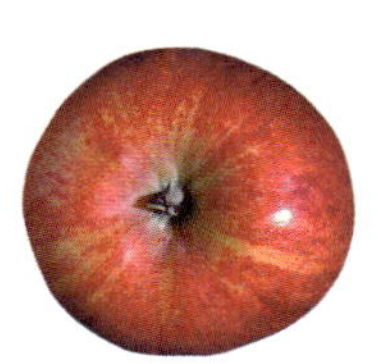 p. 44
**Apple**
- Apfel
Revolution 60°
2014-05-01

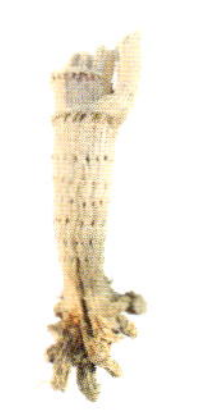 p. 28/29
**Pumpkin**
- Kürbispflanze
3 ½ Revolutions
2019-07-28

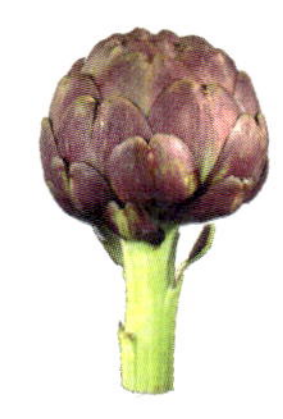 p. 37
**Artichoke**
- Artischocke
Revolution 210°
2017-04-17

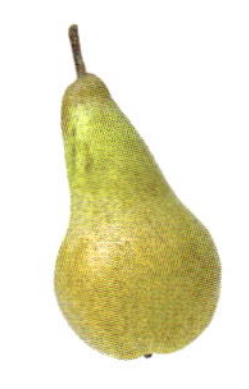 p. 45
**Pear**
- Birne
Revolution 180°
2018-01-27

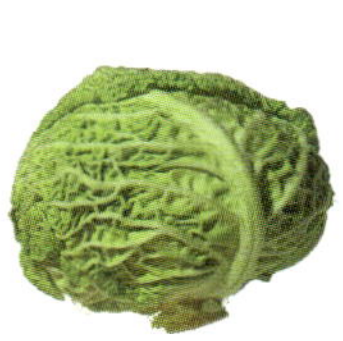 p. 30/31
**Savoy cabbage**
- Wirsingkohl
1 ½ Revolutions
2014-04-20

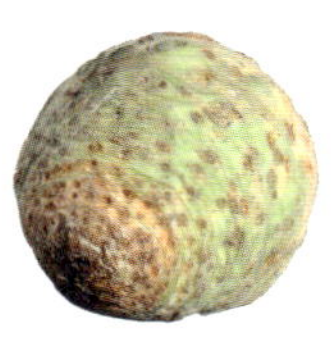 p. 38/39
**Celery root**
- Knollensellerie
Revolution 270°
2013-01-12

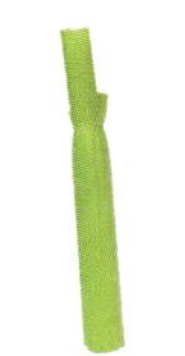 p. 46/47
**Celery stalk**
- Stangensellerie
6 Revolutions
2019-03-06

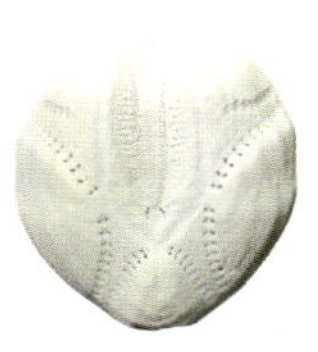 p. 32
**Sea urchin** (Irregularia)
- Seeigel
2 ½ Revolutions
2020-01-16

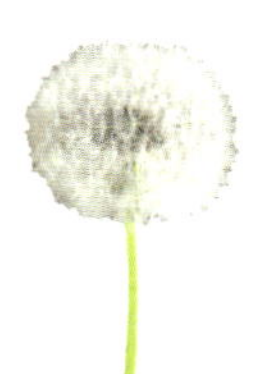 p. 40
**Dandelion** (fruit stand)
- Löwenzahn
1 ½ Revolutions
2016-05-11

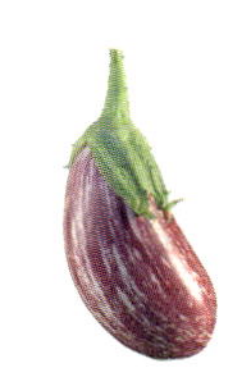 p. 48
**Eggplant** ("Striata")
- Aubergine
1 ½ Revolutions
2018-03-08

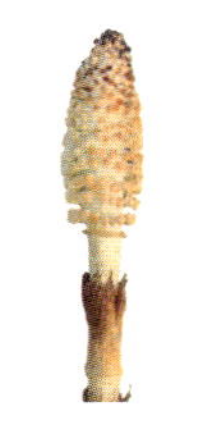 p. 33
**Horsetail** (spore stand)
- Schachtelhalm
8 Revolutions
2020-04-18

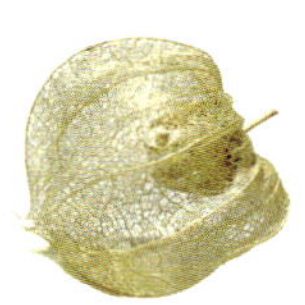 p. 41
**Physalis peruviana**
- Andenbeere
1 ½ Revolutions
2016-04-12

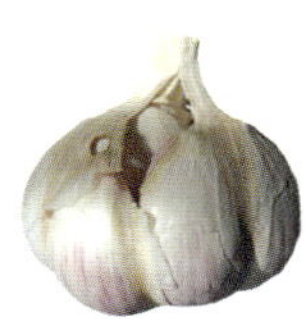 p. 49
**Garlic**
- Knoblauch
Revolution 180°
2013-10-11

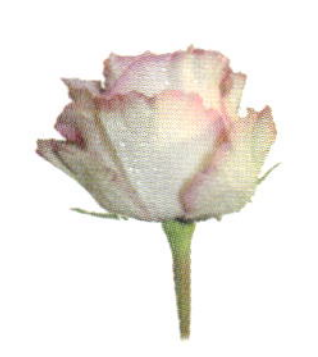 p. 34/35
**Rose blossom**
- Rose
2 Revolutions
2015-03-09

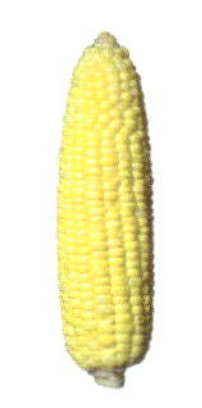 p. 42/43
**Corn on the cob**
- Maiskolben
4 Revolutions
2013-06-09

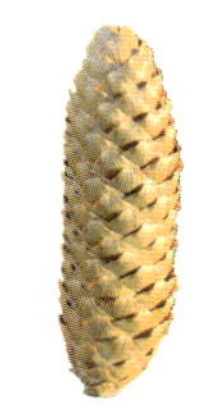 p. 50/51
**Pine cone** (spruce)
- Tannzapfen
2 ½ Revolutions
2020-02-02

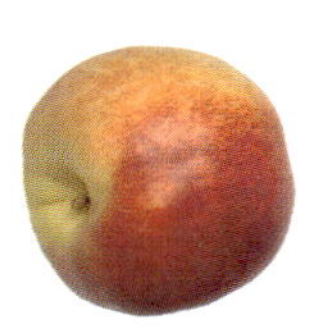

p. 52
**Peach**
- Pfirsich
Revolution 120°
2017-07-24

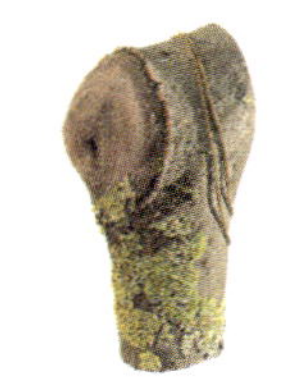

p. 60/61
**Wood with gold chain**
- Holz, Goldkette
Revolution 270°
2020-01-12

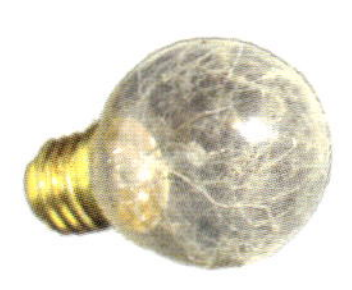

p. 69
**Light bulb**
- Glühbirne
Revolution 180°
2013-08-29

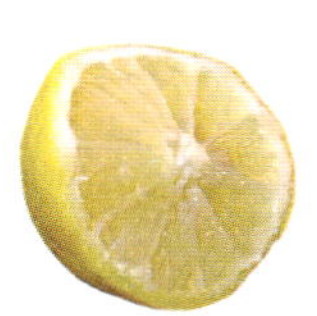

p. 53
**Lemon, cut**
- angeschnittene Zitrone
Revolution 330°
2013-03-30

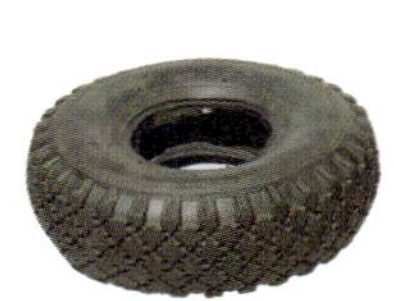

p. 62/63
**Tire**
- Reifen
Revolution 360°
2013-11-17

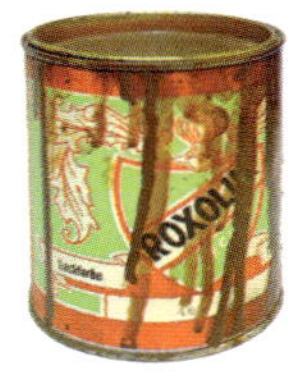

p. 70/71
**Paint can**
- Farbkübel
1 ½ Revolutions
2013-01-19

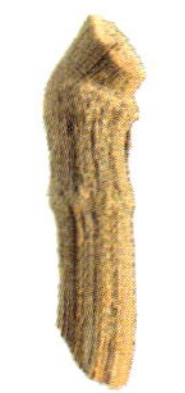

p. 54/55
**Clematis**
- Waldrebe
2 ½ / 4 ½ Revolutions
2020-03-26

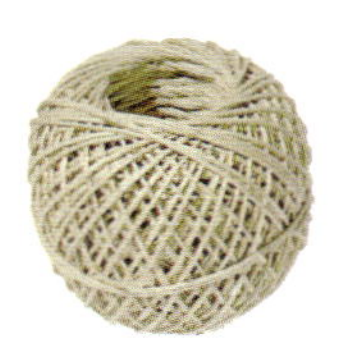

p. 64
**Ball of string**
- Schnurknäuel
Revolution 180°
2014-04-07

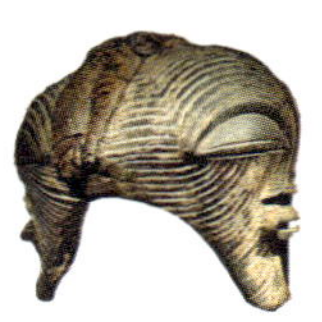

p. 72
**Congolese mask**
- Kongolesiche Maske
No Revolution
2019-12-29

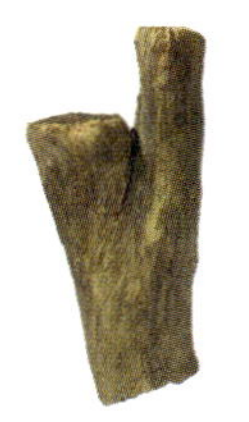

p. 56
**Piece of wood**
- Altholz
1 ¼ Revolutions
2017-11-19

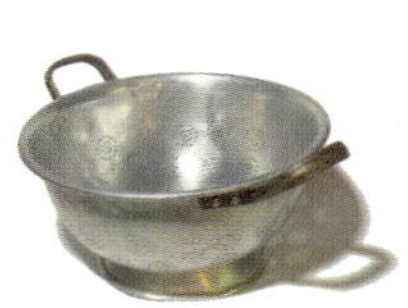

p. 65
**Colander**
- Salatsieb
Revolution 60°
2013-07-04

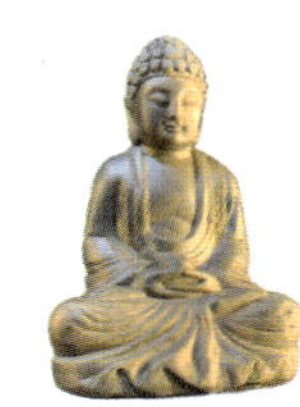

p. 73
**Buddha statue**
- Buddhastatue
1 ½ Revolutions
2020-03-05

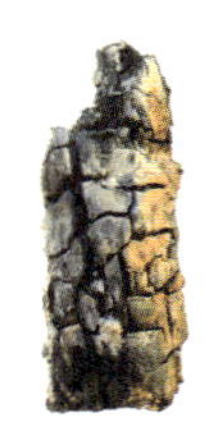

p. 57
**Charcoal**
- Holzkohle
1 ¼ Revolutions
2020-04-12

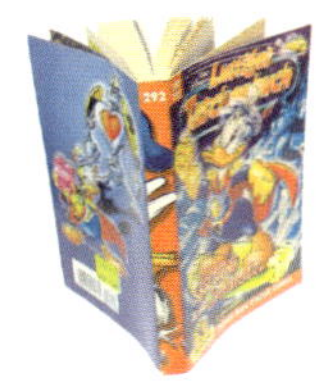

p. 66/67
**Comic book**
- Comicbuch
2 ½ Revolutions
2015-03-25

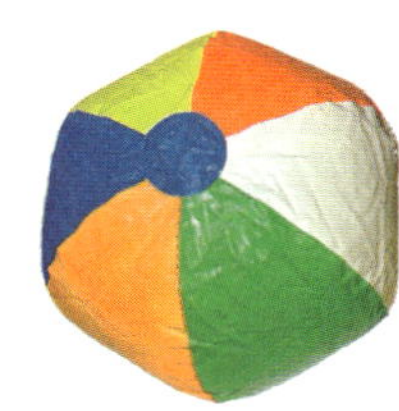

p. 74/75
**Beach ball**
- Wasserball
Revolution 270°
2016-01-31

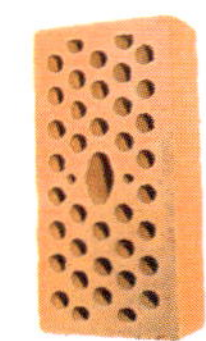

p. 58/59
**Brick**
- Ziegelstein
4 ½ Revolutions
2020-12-28

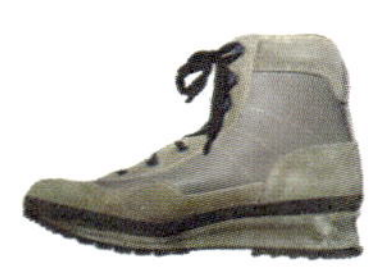

p. 68
**Hiking shoe**
- Bergschuh
Revolution 90°
2013-07-15

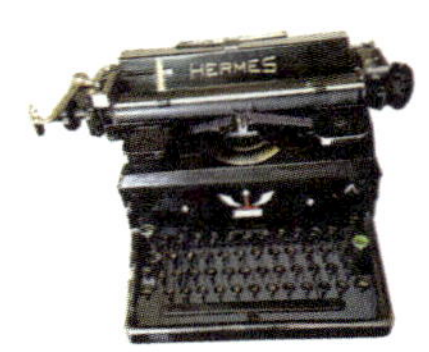

p. 76
**Typewriter**
- Schreibmaschine
Revolution 180°
2014-01-01

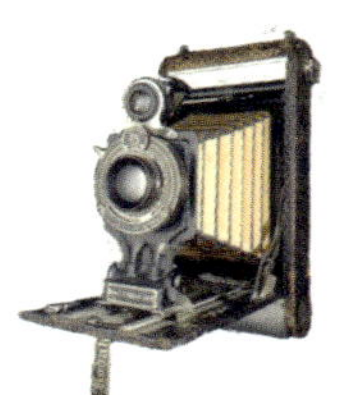

p. 77
**Bellows camera**
- Balgenkamera
1 ½ Revolutions
2019-08-01

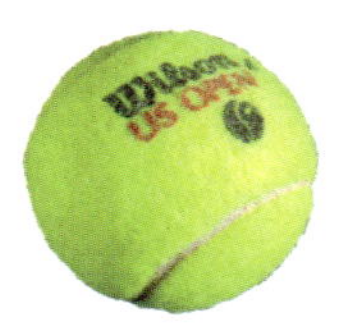

p. 85
**Tennis ball**
- Tennisball
Revolution 150°
2013-09-09

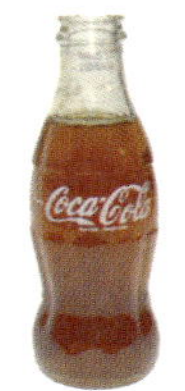

p. 78/79
**Coke bottle**
- Colaflasche
1 ½ Revolutions
2020-03-29

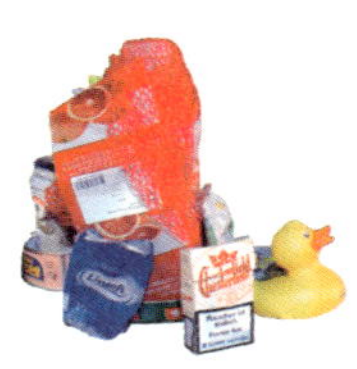

p. 86/87
**Trash still life**
- Stillleben Abfall
1 ½ Revolutions
2017-04-19

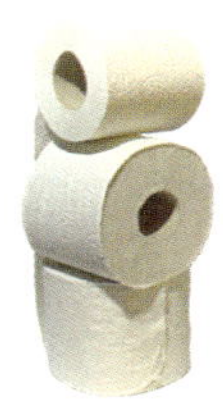

p. 80
**Toilet paper**
- Toilettenpapier
Revolution 180°
2013-11-21

Insgesamt sind über 4200 Aufnahmen entstanden, vor allem von alltäglichen Objekten aus Haushalt und Natur.

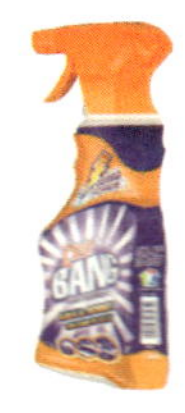

p. 81
**Cleaning agent**
- Putzmittel
1 ½ Revolutions
2016-01-31

In total, more than 4200 photographs were taken, mainly of everyday objects from the household and nature.

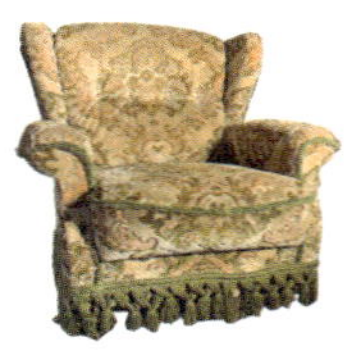

p. 82/83
**Armchair**
- Fauteuil
Revolution 270°
2020-01-20

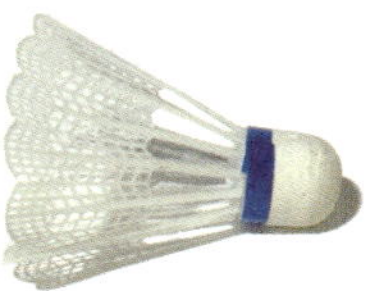

p. 84
**Shuttlecock**
- Federball
1 ½ Revolutions
2013-08-29

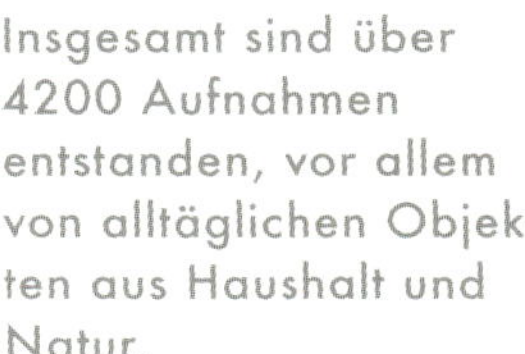